Have I Ever Told You, You're My Favorite!

The Importance of Feeling Special

Paula —
you are magnificently
favored!

Maryann Ehmann, BS, JD

Maryann

Printed in the United States of America

Ehmann, BS, JD, Maryann
    Have I Ever Told You, You're My Favorite! The Importance of Feeling Special/ by Maryann Ehmann, BS, JD

ISBN: 978-0-9826593-0-4

Warning – Disclaimer
The purpose of this book is to educate and entertain. The author or publisher does not guarantee that anyone following the techniques, suggestions, tips, ideas, or strategies will become successful. The author and publisher shall have neither liability or responsibility to anyone with respect to loss or damage caused, or alleged to be caused, directly or indirectly by the information contained in this book.

This book is dedicated to my Pops,

"Sunny,"

Who always has a smile on his face, a twinkle in his eyes,

and a ton of unconditional love to share.

TABLE OF CONTENTS

ACKNOWLEDGEMENTS

Thank you, my God, that You know my heart, and that this little space could not possibly contain all my gratitude. But, I must also thank you for keeping me on Your radar screen, plucking me out of obscurity and vividly showing me I was Yours — 30 years ago! Thank you that I've always been Yours, and even when I denounced You, You did not forget or discard me. Thank you for helping me to love and like myself, thus giving me a greater ability to love others. Thank you for always providing the right people, at the right time, in just the right place, to join me in this grand adventure. And finally, thank you for daily dispelling my doubts, making each day new, and inspiring me to finish this project! I am Yours forever.

Thank you for my husband, my constant cheerleader, my best friend in all the world, the one who keeps my head on straight, and the one who challenges me to stay true to my heart and Your calling. Thank you, my darling, for looking at what others have seen as my flaws, and instead, seeing them as precious qualities — not to be changed, but appreciated. Thank you for always being available to hear the voice of God and to know without a doubt that it is in Him we move and live and have our being. I am so grateful to be on this journey with you.

Maryann Ehmann, BS, JD

A special thanks to all my children, Rebecca and Matthew, Nicole and Eric, Rachel, and Joe.

You all have given my life meaning in a way I never thought possible. Without you, I would never have known what it's really like to love with a whole heart. Thank you for changing my life and letting me share it with the world. You are all my favorites, my bright and shining stars! Oh, how I love you all.

Thank you for all my family and friends. Throughout the process of writing this book, I have become so aware of all of you — the people who love, support, and believe in me. Thank you, dear ones. I am overwhelmed.

Thank you for my new friend, Georgina Chong-You, for her excellent service in editing this book. Georgina, God has gifted you with anointed eyes to see things many of us can't. Thank you for your speedy response and working under such a tight timeframe.

FOREWORD

We all have a message . . . you know, something that pours out of us, almost reflexively. It is always something for which we have passion. It is something that everyone, with whom we have more than the briefest contact, will hear about. We must tell them!

Maryann can speak authoritatively about many issues. Her professional life has been varied and spectacular! As a lawyer, teacher, independent business person, life coach, partner with a successful private investigator, and now author, her passion could be about many things. Her message could be about relationships, as a daughter, wife, mother, grandmother, or friend, but here in *Have I Ever Told You, You're My Favorite?*, her message, her passion, is from God and it's for you!

Not in some vague fashion but specifically about connecting with God's heartfelt desire for you to know without doubt, that He completely and totally accepts you, esteems you, and favors you. You are His favorite! You are special.

Maryann Ehmann, BS, JD

This is not some romp in the world of self-esteem; that topic has been done to death. As a minister for over thirty years, I have seen the emptiness of and harm done to men and women who want so desperately to know that they are loved, that they are accepted unconditionally, that in fact, they do have favor — and yet they *don't, or, can't* appropriate it. If that is you, Maryann will skillfully guide you, in a thoughtful yet practical and engaging way, to understand the abundant supply of favor available to you, identify minor and major resistance, and allow its transforming power to change your life.

Many will find the unique presentation of these principles to be new ground, never traveled, in their lives. Others, who have heard these principles but have never found the keys to their release, *will* find them. For the rest, it will be a welcome reminder, a refresher course, which will reinvigorate the power of favor in our lives. So this book *is* for you. Maryann's message, her passion, is clear. Come, read and experience life!

John J. Ebel, Pastor and friend
Hamlin New Testament Church
Hamlin, NY

INTRODUCTION

Wouldn't you agree, being someone's favorite makes us feel special? Having favor shine upon us can change our lives! And while favor is not all that is necessary to fulfill our dreams, in every success story, we see it is an essential piece of the puzzle.

The story of Michael Oher, as portrayed in the hit movie, "**Blind Side**," demonstrates this point beautifully.

Here's a young man who grew up in the "mean streets of northern Memphis," one of 13 children born to a drug addicted mom and a father who was murdered. Forced to fend for himself at the "ripe old age" of 6 or 7, Michael slept on his front porch, was in and out of eleven schools in nine years, and repeatedly ran away from every foster home he was put in.

In the movie, poverty stricken Michael, appears to *just happen* to be enrolled in an elite private Christian school, and *just happen* to catch on to athletics, and *just happen* to cross the path of the Tuohy's, the now famous, well-to-do Caucasian family who took Michael in as their own and turned him into a star.

But upon closer inspection into Michael's life, we can see that there were no accidents, no happenstances, no luck. Yes, forces converged at just the right moments, with just the right people, in just the right places, but it was no coincidence.

Those right moments, people, and places are what is called *favor*. And it is waiting for us all.

Why? Because we are all created for a reason. We all have God-given dreams and a specially designed destiny. Favor isn't just a nice thing that comes along once in a while randomly. It is a necessity to living the life for which we were intended.

Indeed, Bill Johnson, a hugely popular pastor of one of the most successful churches in America, says this:

> **"Our authentic dreams from God cannot be accomplished on our own. That is a sure sign that a dream is too small. We must dream so big that without the support that comes through *favor* with God and man, we could never accomplish what is in our hearts."[1]**

We need favor.

WE ARE ALL SOMEONE'S FAVORITE

You see, we are all someone's favorite. And thankfully, we don't have to depend on man, who tends to be a bit on the fickle side, but rather, we can depend on God. **Favor begins with God.** Favor flows through God. And it is God who puts it in the hearts of people to extend favor, one to another, whether we recognize it as Him or not.

Too often, our opinion about God is that of a harsh, mean taskmaster or one who is uninvolved with and indifferent about our daily lives. This view of Him totally obscures the favor that He consistently and repeatedly surrounds us with.

But He knows our inability to see sometimes, and even in opening our eyes, we are given favor to see. We need His constant involvement. We need His favor. Thankfully, He loves us with an immeasurable, incomparable love that is so immense that it actually takes revelation to fully realize.

Often God has spoken to my heart and said, "Maryann, if only you knew just how much I love you... you would have no fears. My love for you is so complete, so satisfying, so hopeful, so good. Things will come your way and try to buffet you, but remember, you have My insulation around you. I will keep you warm, and help you through. I am with you. You have My favor. Do not fear."

The more I know God, the more clearly I see and feel His love for me, and oddly enough, the more I am aware of His favor wherever I go.

It's a lovely thing to walk into a room of strangers, or into a new setting, or take on a challenging project, confident that God's favor is there for you.

FAVOR TO IMPACT ANOTHER'S LIFE
People who embrace the favor of God are much more readily available to extend that favor to others. For a while, as you are just learning about favor, and allowing yourself to be the object of it, you may just be focused on the receiving of it, rather than the giving of it.

But favor has a natural flow to it. Sooner or later, you will find yourself compelled to bless another with it.

I believe that is where the Tuohy's were. It is clear their faith in God was an instrumental part of their daily lives. Their business success and wholesome family attitudes reflect the lives of people who live in the favor of God.

Maryann Ehmann, BS, JD

I dare say, they were confident of it. "Blessed to be a blessing," was clearly and powerfully evident and it changed Michael's whole life.

WE ARE ALL MEANT TO BE SOMEBODY

Michael is living his dream now, playing in the NFL. Probably he was living way beyond his dream when he accepted the help and love of the Tuohy's.

But there's another hidden aspect of Michael's story ...

Did you know that he would dream of playing in the NFL as a kid? That at 10 years old he would watch the game on TV and study it? That he would *say* each day, "I'm going to work hard to get to this next goal?"

How does a kid with his background, raised in the deadbeat, drug and crime infested neighborhood from which he came, come up with that? Somehow in the middle of all of that, he had a dream. And even more, he believed that somehow, someway, *he* could achieve it. Clearly he did not map out a plan of action, and set specific timely goal points. But he intuitively sensed that if he did nothing, he would get nowhere.

While no one was looking, Michael was looking out for his own future. Being the size he was, he could have easily secured a position as a bodyguard for one of the many gang leaders. But no, Michael knew he was made for more.

In one of his many interviews, he said, "I wanted to be *something* in life. I didn't want to hang out and do drugs." Deep within his soul, Michael knew, without a doubt, that he was different. He was *special*.

I am convinced that believing in himself and knowing he was special was essential to Michael even going on. It gave him his vision, his strength, and his determination to which he could apply to his God-given talent.

I happen to believe God had favor on Michael, and put that dream, as well as talent, in his heart. Seeing how God has worked in others' lives, including my own, the notion that **I can be someone**, is planted in the hearts of us all. We are all meant to be someone — someone special. Someone who makes a difference in this world. We are set up to impact the world. To have dreams and achieve them. So much so, that even cruelty, abuse, prejudice and neglect cannot keep many of us down. There is something so powerful in each of us that is made to rise up and overcome all obstacles, and that something is love. **Favor emanates from love.**

ARE YOU READY?
One secret of success in life is for a man to be ready for his opportunity when it comes.
–Benjamin Disraeli

At various points of time, Michael's life looked anything but favored. But does the station and position of our life determine whether we have favor or not? Thankfully, no.

Michael says that he always did what needed to be done, whether using the front porch as a mattress, begging neighbors for takeout, or breaking out of foster homes. "Whatever it took to get to the following sunrise." Determination was definitely part of his skill set.

I know this begs the question, "Why did he rise above the rubble and others didn't? Why did he have this favor fall upon him, not others?" I believe clearly that everyone has it, but what we do with it is what makes the difference. One of the goals of this book is to increase your awareness of favor and receptivity to it.

It is clear, favor can often be overlooked, rejected, or taken for granted. Sometimes we just aren't ready for it. However, it is there when we need it. We can count on it. But to maximize it, we need to be ready and prepare for it.

Michael was ready for it. Maybe he didn't know it or define it as I am now, but he took the favor he had, which was his attitude, beliefs, and talent, and he worked with it to the degree he could.

But Michael would need lots more favor, love, and caring before he could fully realize his potential.

Before the Tuohys came along, another generous man, Tony Henderson, picked out Michael and mentored him. Tony, even today, is a man who mentors the teens in Michael's old neighborhood, Hurt Village, providing a much-needed service: father figure.

Describing Michael as a "great kid, a quiet kid," Tony saw the potential in Michael and along with his own son, enrolled him in Briarcrest, a private Christian school. Though hesitant and leery, the administration gave Michael a chance to get a quality education when he had had none, as well as the opportunity to use his athleticism, if his grades allowed.

It was there that the Tuohys met Michael, gave him a place to live, and eventually adopted him as their own. One piece of favor, leading to another, which led to another.

Michael was so ready. A kid with a dream, talent, and hard core determination converges in time with the right people, at the right time, in the right place, all necessary elements to him reaching his goals.

Are you ready?

HOW TO BE READY

Being convinced you are loved, special, and have favor will go a long way to getting you ready. Do you know that you are as loved, as special, and as favored as Michael?

Do you realize that favor comes from the pulsating heart of God, who loves you passionately? Do you know that He has already given it to you, and it's yours to know, embrace, and operate in **your** life?

If you don't know your purpose, are unclear about your dreams, or don't have a clue about your destiny, you are missing out on a huge chunk of life for which you have been created. Seek God, ask for help, or obtain guidance. I have figured out much of this by sitting quietly in the presence of God, and listening to His voice. I can show you how easy and rewarding this is. In addition, there are plenty of wonderful coaches out there that are qualified to help you.

Once you access what it is you are called to do or discover your purpose, get the additional skills and knowledge, if you don't already have them. Chances are you do. They are just waiting to be repurposed.

Furthermore — develop discipline, determination, focus, and passion. These are all important ingredients to your success.

But in the process of it all, approach everything with an awareness and expectation of favor. **At a minimum, you need to know and feel you are <u>God's</u> favorite, and dare I say, that would be a most profitable origination point? You need to be convinced that you are special in this world.**

Obstacles will be there in abundance. There is an evil force in this world that opposes God and His children. These obstacles will obscure your vision and trick your mind into believing the lie that you don't matter, and no one cares.

This little book is meant to help you gain full assurance that you are God's favorite. That concept, fully embraced, will open your eyes to opportunities where favor abounds. There are few confidence builders more effective than favor.

Through my own and others' stories of favor, interactive exercises, and scriptural support, favor will be second nature to you. Eventually, it will be a natural part of your being.

Michael Oher's success was due to a combination of focus, determination, a little help, and a lot of love. Well, there is a lot of love waiting to be released in the form of favor for you.

Come with me and learn what it is, why you have it, and how to live in the realm of it. You will love it.

We're All Someone's Favorite!

There is much confusion surrounding the word, favor. Many times I, and others I have spoken to, have been puzzled, and even resistant, about this deeply significant subject.

The idea that "favor is mine" was not one I accepted easily. I needed the Lord to show me over and over incidences along my life's journey where I had missed it. I needed to see it for myself in His eyes and hear it in His words. I needed to search the Bible and find it repeatedly in order for me to give myself the permission to believe it.

Awakening to favor, and then being convinced, took a while, and was so personal, that I was very reluctant to share it with anyone.

Recently my friend, Dee, and I were discussing my hesitation. I shared with her the blank looks I often encounter when I bring up the topic of favor. Clearly people were not getting what I meant.

As my good friend, who thoroughly supports me in most everything I do, she took the word favor to the Lord, asking Him, "Lord, is there something favor equals so people will understand?"

She quickly saw that His death for us was quite a favor, and that resonated with her, but then to her amazement, she heard Him say, "Have I ever told you, <u>you're</u> My favorite?"

"Oh, my. I'm you're favorite?" In an instant, Dee's eyes were opened to God's favor ... for her, personally. Being rooted in much neglect and rejection while growing up, Dee often struggled to believe that she truly was a person of true worth and value. While she had fought hard for that truth and won, being God's favorite never entered her mind. This was a life changing, favored exchange, flowing from Dee's heart, to God's and then out of His, and straight back into hers. Lovely.

For days after, Dee felt the penetrating reverberations of His special touch, causing her heart to swell and her spirit to elevate whenever she thought upon it. We can be sure that this will become a memory to Dee, as significant and powerful as any she has ever had with her husband, her children, or special friends.

Besides lifting her spirits though, God's voice to Dee served another monumental purpose. During this time, Dee and her family were one of the many casualties of the recession, and after much prayerful consideration, they decided to give up their home. After a long period of uncertainty, a buyer was found, and a deal was struck. Finally, they were on their way to the next phase of their life.... Except for some dang paperwork that was holding up the whole process, possibly even threatening the deal.

Dee called and together we prayed and agreed the favor of God was hers and would work to their benefit. Within a day, the plug in the process had been removed. All pieces fell into place, and the next step could be taken.

I love being able to participate in the operation of favor. I am continually fueled by the joy I see in people's faces when they know they have just been blessed by God. Favor has power.

Through Dee's example, and others like her, I have become absolutely convinced that it is God's design that mankind know, understand, and embrace His favor. Notice — she merely asked and He provided, in her heart and practically, in her situation. This is not just an ethereal, Kumbaya experience.

Being turned on and enlightened to favor is one of most compelling, effective, and enjoyable lessons of life.

With your cooperation, God will bring forward memories, maybe long forgotten, or in need of the His slant on it, memories where favor was operating, where you were someone's favorite. In Chapter 3 you will have an opportunity to engage some of those memories.

One such memory brought forward by the Lord for me involved my grandfather…

I was his favorite. I think everyone suspected that, but I knew it because he told me often. Being someone's favorite has its privileges! Riding around in his new, shiny red convertible, top down, wind blowing in my face, accompanying him to his local hangout, sitting in the booth with his arm around me, and drinking Shirley Temples with his old cronies — that was special. Having him pay for my first two years of college, room and board, and a brand new car. To a 17 year old kid, that was **really** special.

But the benefit I loved the most was the pride in his eyes when he looked at me — I can't even describe the extraordinary joy that I felt.

For years, I relished the idea that I was also my dad's favorite. I loved how he paid attention to me when I talked, and always had this appreciative smile in his eyes. It wasn't until I was in my 20's that I realized all his children felt that same way. Somehow he was able to convey to the six of us that we were all his favorites and not reduce the specialness of it.

Though my dad and my grandfather were not perfect, and we children had to endure many difficulties growing up, being special and feeling favored, did much to help us carry a more carefree, happy attitude through it all.

In another excerpt from Bill Johnson's *Face to Face with God*, he quotes from the book, *Living From The Heart Jesus Gave You*:

".... some neurologists now say that the basic human need is to be the **"sparkle in someone's eye."** When you catch a glimpse of a child's face as she **runs toward** an awaiting parent with arms outstretched in unrestrained joy, you can witness firsthand the **incredible power that comes from "being the sparkle in someone's eye."** When this joy is the strongest force in a child's world, life makes sense because children look forward to moments when they can re-connect to joy - by being with their beloved. Wonderfully enough, that innocent, pure desire that begins in childhood continues through our life. Life makes sense and is empowered by joy when people are in relationship with those who love them and are **sincerely "glad to be with them."**

Johnsons goes on to conclude, "This reveals why so many struggle with the subject of joy in the church. And more importantly, it shows why most have so little joy in their personal lives ....**They've not seen the favor and approval from their heavenly Father."**[2]

David, shepherd turned king, was known to be 'the apple of God's eye." In the Psalms, we see the depth and intimacy he had with the Almighty. As awesome and fearsome as God is, David felt an uncanny safety being in His presence. Knowing, believing, and embracing such favor makes us feel safe, protected, and extremely blessed.

FAVORITISM, THE UGLY COUSIN TO FAVOR

I don't want to spend a lot of time on this, but it is worth mentioning that **favoritism is favor gone sour**. It often involves the preferential treatment on one person or group to the disadvantage of another. It may be why people have a hard time fully embracing the genuine thing. Either they have been hurt by favoritism or have felt guilty being the chosen, favored one.

I've experienced both.

I was a slanty-eyed kid in an all white world. At first I thought nothing of it. Even the stares, the 'ching chongs', and the frequent pulling up on the corners of my mocker's eyes didn't do much to spoil my day. But the feeling that I always had to beg people to let me play, participate, or join in, did. I never attributed it to maybe … prejudice. But over time I got the message. It was not cool to look like me. Favoritism toward others often excluded me. (Happily, God has corrected my negative view of myself!)

The example of my grandfather had elements of favoritism which caused me to feel guilty. Yes, it had its advantages, but as I got older, I realized it was unfair to my siblings. I also felt worried that they would be angry with me. This kept me from fully enjoying his favor.

FAVOR FROM MAN CAN OFTEN BE A DOUBLE-EDGED SWORD.

Thankfully, God's favor is pure and for us all, in greater measure than we can use in one life time! He has plenty to go around, and desires to liberally distribute it. It flows out of the "sparkle" in His eyes for each of us.

So, now you may be asking, "Am I anyone's favorite? Have I ever been anyone's favorite?" Well, I can say without equivocation, a resounding, "YES!" But my telling you will not be good enough. You have to find out for yourself. Start by asking God to shine His light of favor on your memories, and even people and events today. Like Dee, ask Him to open your eyes to it. He will be more than happy to do so!

PRAYER:

FATHER, WHO KNOWS ALL AND SEES ALL, I GIVE YOU PERMISSION TO DIG DEEP IN MY MEMORY AND SHOW ME A TIME WHEN I WAS SOMEONE'S FAVORITE. HELP ME TO SEE CLEARLY THAT I AM ALWAYS YOURS!

WRITE YOUR MEMORY:

_____

_____

_____

_____

2

MY ROAD TO FAVOR, THE JOURNEY HOME

Universally, being someone's favorite makes us feel special. It isn't important if we are the only favorite or one of many favorites, just as long as the message that "we are special" gets conveyed. Feeling special gives us a measure of hope, encouragement, and energy. It touches our hearts and makes us feel loved, like we matter. And really, isn't that the point?

I believe almost all of us start off in life being favored, the sparkle in someone's eye. Every little thing we did as a child brought a cheer, or a smile, or a "Did you see what she just did?"

I'll never forget the first time I held my little baby. Wonderment, ecstasy, and penetrating peace filled my heart. I couldn't stop staring at her, marveling at her beauty. As the days and months passed, I delighted in every new discovery about her personality, her likes and dislikes, the way she advanced through various stages of development at lightening speed. (She crawled up a flight of stairs at five months old, tried to stand, and plummeted down onto the slate floor below. The first of many falls she would survive with nary a scratch.)

For an infant, up until they become toddlers, the world is, as they say, their oyster! Carefree loving, learning, playing, and exploring... these are their main jobs in life. This is a wonderful state of favor! Even those who come from dysfunctional families have elements of this.

But as time goes on, favor begins to be eroded. We become less carefree. We begin to believe certain lies about who we are, who God is, and what we can expect in this world. We become disillusioned, discouraged, and for some, downright depressed. Cynicism becomes a way for us to guard our hearts against any further disappointments.

I was born into a quite a favored life. With Korean, Italian, and Polish parents, our lives were rich with cultural diversity. We lived in beautiful custom built homes, always had more than enough food, plenty of clothes, toys, and opportunities.

My grandfather delighted us with his ukulele, teaching us how to sing songs like "Oye Marie" and "That's Amore." He was a colorful and animated character, yelling more than he talked, especially when it came to making the sauce. (For you Italians out there… you know what I'm talking about.)

My sweet grandma, always under Grandpa's thumb, often secretly slipped us $20 bills when he wasn't looking, loaded us with treats, and spoiled us rotten. We loved going to the Echo Club with my aunties and uncles for parties and, tearing up the dance floor with our version of the polka. I often chuckle reflecting on that scene … Little Asian kids dancing the polka … Priceless.

My beautiful mom, originally from Hawaii, had grown up in poverty and had to quit school early to work in the pineapple plantations. For years this made her feel inadequate. Having also suffered multiple abuses, rejection and abandonment up through her teens, shame and guilt were her steady, silent companions, and it would be decades before she would feel free of their power.

After she married my dad and moved to western NY, she was ill-equipped to handle the onslaught of prejudice. This was the 50's and smack dab in the middle of the Korean War. Not very good timing.

Nevertheless, my mom had a great sense of humor, and the most infectious laugh. How she would throw her head back and release herself to the moment! I'm sure it was her saving grace.

To keep her culture alive, she had Hawaiian luaus, made us take hula lessons, introduced us to Kim chi and Kalbi and, of course, served rice at every meal. Like all good Asian moms, she was more than diligent to teach us how to work hard, be disciplined, and strive for a better life. For her, the secret to success lied in higher education. Period.

My dad was kind and compassionate, and often the one that made us pee our pants from laughing so hard. Not just the funny man, he promoted lively dinner conversations about life, the power of positive thinking, and the innate value of people. After dinner and clean up, we would often charge to the living room where Dad would tickle the ivories, with spontaneous renditions of "boogie-woogie." What a gas it was, all of us dancing together, looking more like body slamming than the Jitterbug.

Except for the occasional racial digs, the first ten years of my life were pretty darn good. However, my parents' marriage was becoming more difficult and my mom's homesickness for her family and the beaches were causing bouts of depression. Nonetheless, we children had a number of wonderful diversions, our property being one of our favorites.

Once a working fruit orchard, this property had a chicken coop and a vacant farmhouse, both of which I used with my sisters' willingness, as my school. The rustic barn loaded with cobwebs and traces of hay held its own adventures, but the best was an old, leaky cement mixing trough, which we dragged into the pond as our boat and used to travel to many distant lands. As the days went on, we'd climb the trees, or build a fire and cook some potatoes, or just fall asleep in the tall grasses. I'm not sure Adam and Eve had it any better.

In so many ways, this was an idyllic life.

But it didn't stay so. My parent's dissatisfaction with each other was becoming more visible, and the arguments and fights were escalating in volume and violence.

Then the unthinkable happened — I was sexually abused, turning my life of favor into one of shame and guilt. My innocent childlike view of the world disappeared, and for months after, I couldn't look anyone in the eye, thinking they might see that awful thing that happened to me. Of course, during those times, this was not something anyone talked about, or for which I received any help. I learned to do what most girls of my age and era did – bury it.[3]

As we know today, a thing buried does not make it go away. It's like radioactive material, leaking into the ground, slowly killing healthy organisms. My favored view of life and self were quietly eroding, dying little by little each day. How I perceived myself and my life was beginning to line up with my hidden beliefs: there's something very wrong, undesirable, and unworthy about me.

(This was proven to me over and over again in high school as I tried out for everything available from student council to parts in the plays, to cheerleading. Do you know anyone who ever tried out for cheerleading 2x/year for 4 years and never made the team? We laugh now and marvel at my tenacity.)

Well, eventually my parents did split up, and despite their best intentions and how much they loved us, were incapable at the time of focusing on little else but their own emotional needs and disappointments.

Thankfully, though, I had years under my belt of carefree frivolity, lots of laughter and love, financial stability, and highly involved, doting grandparents that delighted in my presence. This favored existence did well to give me a strong foundation, which I would return to much later.

Despite this strong beginning, I unknowingly allowed guilt and shame to take residence in my soul. This made me a keen observer as I tried to figure out what would keep me safe and make me a worthwhile person.

Two books, now quite famous, came across my path: one, *How to Win Friends and Influence People,*[4] by Dale Carnegie, and the other, *The Power of Positive Thinking,*[5] by Norman Vincent Peale. Oh, how they gave me hope! Every babysitting job was a golden opportunity (once the kiddies went to bed, of course), to study, outline, and memorize these life-giving materials. After my study, I would then take valuable nuggets, copy them down, and post them in my locker in school. I look back at that now and think…who does that at sixteen years of age?

I am aware of the negative thoughts some Christian leaders have toward books like these, but I am convinced they were planted in my path by God Himself, as a concrete life line for my dying soul.

Because I was a natural cheerleader (despite not being invited to join a "real" team) and effective peace maker, I was also every one's confidant. And so, my perceived value in life was attached to making others feel happy and safe.

If they weren't, well, it was somehow my fault. Under my toothy grin and happy-go-lucky attitude, I lived with a perpetual sense of failure.

It would be years before I would understand the dysfunctional nature of that set up, and how it would impact my life, but at 17, I did know that if I was to ever survive this world, I would need to fend for myself, "Get outta Dodge," and become a "somebody".

It is widely accepted that our mental habits, which are the thoughts we habitually think — especially those we are not aware of — dictate the choices we make, the situations we "find ourselves in," and how we experience life. These mental habits create the filter through which we perceive God, ourselves, and our relationship to the world. My filter wasn't so good.

On the "positive side", this perception of being defective and damaged kept me striving to be better, improve, and gain more knowledge and skills. I became the typical ambitious person. Many significant results were produced! I became a teacher when there was a glut in the market, a lawyer when it was highly uncommon for women to do so, and a prosecutor for the most powerful legal agency in the state.

Though I didn't recognize it as such, favor was clearly operating in my life, even in the design of my personality, my education, and diligence, all important factors for my success. Maybe I would have enjoyed the journey more and relaxed a little if I had known about favor, but the only thing that was reinforced was working hard.

As hard as I worked, though, my boss upped the ante, by reminding me that because I was a woman, I would have to work twice as hard and twice as long as my male counterparts.

In today's world, these are fighting words and could possibly get someone fired. But then, we women knew that was the price we had to pay to play with the "big boys." (Another subject for another day!) I did what I had to and in a short time, I was earmarked for the fast track to judgeship.

Despite the momentary bliss of each achievement and recognition however, I reverted back to discontented restlessness. This was not how I thought life would feel once I achieved my goals. As I reviewed my life, I realized that I had partied my way through most everything, relying on drugs and alcohol, and had too many failed relationships — including a marriage, (oh yes, I forget to mention that, didn't I!) Though I hobnobbed with some of the most powerful people in the state, I still felt small, lonely, and insignificant.

Discouragement led to confusion, and for the first time in my life, I experienced something that my "whistle a happy tune" personality did not understand: **depression.** Little did I realize that the pursuit of excellence motivated by unresolved guilt and shame could lead to depressing results.

In the midst of my funk, I went home for a holiday. While languishing on the couch, I felt captive as my sister Cheryl read to me from the Bible. Just when I thought I was about to hiss, spit, and writhe like the demoniac of Gadara, she invited me to go to church with her and her family.

OMG … how could she not remember that I had denounced God and became an atheist nine years prior? But to keep her from reading out of that ancient, irrelevant book, I struck a deal and agreed.

You know, predicting life and controlling its curve balls, was one of my fortes. But in my wildest dreams, I could never have predicted what happened the next morning.

My sister and brother in law's church was actually a room in an office building. What no steeple, stained-glass windows or wooden pews? Well, that threw me off. The people sang without hymnals, or even words on a screen, and that really threw me off. But then, as I listened to them, I could have sworn I heard a choir of angels. I was starting to feel uncomfortable. But not as uncomfortable as I was about to feel.

The pastor's message was all about the Greeks' lust for knowledge and wisdom, and how they thought it was the answer to their salvation. Uh, oh. Was that my problem?

Then the clincher: He told us to take out a coin and read it. "In God We Trust." I had never noticed that before, and before I could finish reading this very short phrase, a stunning thing occurred, "Heaven came down and glory filled my soul."

God interrupted my pity party, having pity on me, and with a mega-volt electrical charge, zapped me into the world of the supernatural, filling me at the cellular level with a love and hope that excited me to the core. This sensation I experienced in my physical body is difficult to describe, but imagine being a hot air balloon let loose during a hurricane of joy. It was exhilarating!

It didn't seem to matter to God that I had given Him no thought, that I never once considered Him to be the missing piece of my life, and that I did not ask for this life altering visitation! **Totally raw, unexpected favor!**

Did you know His love is active, far reaching, and nothing short of miraculous?

Catapulted out of the pit of despair, I was flying, thoroughly enjoying the reality that I belonged to God. Yes, I belong to God! I belong to Somebody! I began to get a glimpse....I really am a somebody! I really do matter. I am special.

This truth is music to the ears of anyone who is plagued with feeling deficient, defective, and guilty. For days, maybe months, I vacillated between fits of laughter and tears of joy, feeling totally fearless and protected.

But the clarity and joy in my heart did not last for long. There was a massive overhaul in my thinking that had to be done, and it was not easy. Little by little God opened my eyes to see the wreckage of my childhood, and how it affected every relationship I had ever been in. Even the thing I had buried was dug up and for a while, looking at it brought me great misery.

I had become cynical and as God revealed the lies upon which I had built my identity, life actually got worse before it got better. As these lies were being dismantled, I did not have replacing truth yet. Often I felt like I was walking a tight rope, and with the slightest breeze I would fall to my death.

But it was during those times that He showed Himself to be Most Faithful, and yes, **I eventually learned how to like and love myself.** In my years of counseling others, I have found liking oneself to be one of the most difficult feats to accomplish, but it is the will of God, and He will help.

I also learned that I did not have to put myself down in order to help others feel more comfortable around me. I learned by elevating others we can all win. I learned that I have precious gifts to offer the world. It has been enjoyable work to embrace and appreciate the beautiful me He created.

In Mt 18:3, Jesus tells us that we need to be able to see and understand as little children, if we are to enter the Kingdom of Heaven. The Kingdom is our real home and it is a place of love, joy, and peace. **It is a place of favor.**

Disillusionment is a block and barrier to seeing as a little child, and often it causes us to settle for a life of skeptical suspicion, cynicism and rejection of the favor God has for us. But see as children we must, if we are ever to live the life to which we have been called: Abundant Life, the one Jesus won for us.

PRAYER:

DEAR FATHER, I DESIRE TO SEE AS A LITTLE CHILD, TO HAVE EYES OF FAITH THAT I AM INDEED PRECIOUS, FAVORED, AND DELIGHTFUL IN YOUR SIGHT. WORK IN ME SO MY VIEW OF MYSELF AGREES WITH YOURS. THANK YOU.

SO, JUST WHAT IS FAVOR, EXACTLY?

"I believe the failure to understand and pursue the journey
of stewarding the favor of God has led so many people to
die in the <u>unnecessary</u> tragedy of never having their
God-given dreams and desires fulfilled"[6]

Yes, not having our God-given dreams and desires fulfilled is indeed an unnecessary tragedy. Especially since God's favor is active and at work in all of our lives, and He is so willing to increase it.

I was blind to favor, focusing too much on my fears, inadequacies, and flaws. Have you ever heard the phrase, "What we focus on expands?" If we focus on the negative, what will expand and operate in our lives? Conversely, if we focus on favor…. Yeah, you got it.

So, let's expand in favor by focusing on what it is and what it isn't.

First, favor does not mean a problem-free life. It does not mean nothing bad will ever happen to you. I know this seems obvious, but after discovering the significance of this gift, I mistakenly assumed everything would go well, all the time.

Interestingly, it mostly did!

But then one day as I was preparing for an upcoming women's retreat, I was hit with some very bad news. Not to be daunted, I believed for a favorable outcome *of my design*. It did not turn out as I thought it should, which led to great confusion and even apprehension on my part. Eventually things worked out well, but not as I had it orchestrated in my mind.

As I looked back over those months, I realized that the Lord used the challenges associated with the event to raise the question, *"Will you believe you are favored, even if things don't look favorable? Is favor merely random and circumstantial or is it a reliable condition of your life from which you are to move?"*

I sought the Lord for His wisdom during this emotional time, and faithfully, He drew my attention to Joseph in the Bible.[7] Joseph was favored by his earthly and Heavenly Father. Given a coat like none other, dreams by God to predict the future, and a pretty cushy life, Joseph was secure in that favor. But he was not without his share of problems.

Thrown in a pit by his jealous brothers, picked up by slave traders, falsely accused by his boss' wife and then imprisoned for three years does not sound like favor. But the story doesn't end there. Even in jail, Joseph prospered and ultimately was instrumental in saving the Egyptian civilization as well as the nation of Israel.

This account along with others broadened my view and deepened my conviction. No matter what, we have the favor of God, and from that, if we need it, we will have the favor of man. We can only anticipate the good — we are made to be secure in His love and provision.

While none of us have trouble-free lives, *favor gives all of us the capacity to triumph.*

SO, WHAT IS FAVOR?

The Merriam-Webster dictionary[8] defines favor as:

1. friendly regard shown toward another especially by a superior
2. approving consideration or attention
3. gracious kindness; *also* **:** an act of such kindness <did you a favor>
4. effort in one's behalf or interest **:** attention
5. a token of love or a small gift or decorative item given out at a party
6. a special privilege or right granted or concede

To be someone's favorite does not mean you are the only one who will receive special attention, and thus it is unavailable for anyone else. This is often the objection to favor: I win — you lose, or you get it — I don't.

Rather, to be a favorite means to be one that is treated or regarded with special favor or liking; a person who is especially loved, trusted, or provided with favors by someone of high rank or authority. *Especially* loved does not of necessity mean *exclusively* loved.

So, now with a more expanded view of favor, consider: Have there ever been times when you had someone's approval, or they gave you a special privilege, or gracious kindness? If after thinking of it, you still think not, then may I encourage you to find out why? I dare say, there are beliefs operating in you that need to be changed.

PRAYER:

LORD, PLEASE DRAW OUT OF MY MEMORIES TIMES, PLACES, OR PEOPLE WHERE I EXPERIENCED FAVOR. SHED YOUR LIGHT ON THE CIRCUMSTANCE OR SITUATION AND GIVE ME A NEW VIEW. THANK YOU!

Use these memory joggers to help you remember times of favor. Take the time to do this and you will be amazed at how much favor you have had.

1. Think of a time when someone in a superior position — whether work, school, and/or organization with which you were associated — showed you friendly regard.

   _____

   _____

2. Has anyone ever approved of what you did, think of you with approval, or give you attention because they approved of you?

   _____

   _____

3. Has anyone ever extended gracious kindness to you, or done you a favor?

_____

_____

4. When has someone paid attention to you or made the effort to bless you, treat you, or benefit you?

_____

_____

5. Have you ever been given a token of love, a small gift, or something that made you feel special?

_____

_____

6. When have you been granted a special privilege, the right to something, or preferential treatment?

_____

_____

4

FAVOR IS GOD'S IDEA

The fact that some people do some crazy, obnoxious, or even harmful things to stand out to make themselves feel special and important, does not mean we are to deny the necessity of this need. Indeed, if we were to accept it as a very real need, and then look to God and His favor, we would have less trouble fulfilling it!

But all too often we throw the baby out with the bath water, even judging others when we see evidence of their attempts. Sometimes our response is, "Well, they just need to be taken down a notch. They need to be humbled!"

Be careful of this thinking! Genuine humility has nothing to do with humiliation. It is not God's way to make us feel insignificant and worthless.

Rather, God has done a great deal, and continues doing so, to show us that we are undeniably special, and have inestimable worth, especially to Him. He is good!!

Joel Osteen, "America's most popular pastor," is a man deeply committed to helping people believe the best about themselves and understand they have the favor of God. Unfortunately, this often subjects him to frequent public criticism.

But favor is not Pastor Osteen's idea! It's God's!

Beginning with Adam and Eve, we see all the definitions of favor in full operation![9]

Let's review:

- Friendly regard
- Approving consideration or attention
- Gracious kindness
- Effort in one's behalf
- Token of love
- Special privilege or right granted

When God created day and night, heaven and earth, and animals and plants, He "saw that it was good."[10] Good. Not sort of good. Good. As we see, *favor has to do with approval.*

Maybe you know that feeling. You know, you've just created a piece of art, made a gourmet meal, or a home-spun craft. You stand back and take a moment to appreciate, smile, and say, "This is good."

Not too long ago, I wanted to redecorate a few rooms in our house. The carpets were disgusting, the walls a boring white, and the furniture tattered from frisky kittens. Decorating had never been my forte and so, I asked the Lord for help. (Isn't it great we can do that?) Almost immediately, three words popped into my mind: Stunning, Serene, and Simple. Perfect. These three words guided all my ideas and purchases, from the deep brick orange on the walls, to the elegant, but durable teak flooring, to the comfy new sectional. When it was done, I looked and said, "Yep. This is good." Maybe nowhere near the creation of the earth and universe, but my creation gave me a small taste and appreciation for what my Maker must have felt.

God was satisfied with His work, thus far, but He wasn't content to stop there.

He still had His masterpiece to make, which is us. Unlike anything else, when God created man and woman, He created them in His likeness, in His image. Then He blessed them, telling them to be fruitful and multiply, giving them this lovely place and all in it to care for.

Talk about extending *effort in one's behalf, special privilege, and preferential treatment.* He certainly did not bless the animals in the same way, and yet He provided for their care, as well!

After specifically recounting all He had generously given to Adam and Eve, again, He stepped back, took it all in, and in obvious delight, thought or said, "Indeed, it was VERY good." [11]

Could *"approving consideration"* be any more evident? This isn't just about Adam and Eve. It's also about us. Favor.

This is a God whose heart is full. Our God — creating, giving, providing, and blessing. All of it to Him was VERY good.

Ponder the beauty of that for a minute. Ask God to open your eyes to see how it matters to you, personally. Do you not feel more significant and precious in His sight?

Now, would you take a moment and think.

We are all familiar with Adam and Eve's fall, how that fall spoiled the whole picture, and made it difficult for the rest of mankind. But has their disobedience caused you to lose sight of God's original intent and the nature of His heart?

Has that been the focus of the story so as to ruin or hamper your expectations?

For years it has been taught that because of their fall and Satan's presence in the world, there is only so much we can expect. And yet, wasn't it Christ who said He came to give life and give it abundantly?[12] Isn't He the One who encouraged us that what would be impossible with man would be possible with God?[13] This is a no-limits, no-hindrance, no nonsense God who is serious about restoring us to favor, to even an Eden experience.

"Thy kingdom come, ON EARTH as it is in HEAVEN."[14] This is Christ's intention and plan, but often it takes our agreement to manifest and experience personally. Thankfully today many are living in this reality, and the harvest of healing, deliverance, prosperity, and increase are being vibrantly displayed in all parts of the world.

The fact that you are reading this book tells me that you want to be a part of this widespread move of God, too. You want to witness miracles in your life, too. You want to vividly see the favor of God in operation for you.

If your mind drifts off into the Land of Limits, ask God to renew it. Let's encourage each other to look upon God clearly, as a God of goodness and kindness toward us, a God who loves to generously give, and sets us up in favorable conditions. To think otherwise is to let a filter of fear and unworthiness cloud the truth.

Our God is a good God, and as one pastor is known for saying, "He is in a good mood today!"

FAVOR IN THE OLD TESTAMENT

Throughout the OT, we see the liberal operation of favor. A common request was, "If I have found favor in your sight....." People understood the absolute necessity for favor in order for many pivotal things to be done.

Abraham asked for the favor of the Lord to not pass him by. "My Lord, if now *I have found favor in thy sight*, pass not away, I pray you, from thy servant." Showing such favor, the Lord stayed and announced that Sarah, though she was old, would give birth to a baby. (Gen 18:3)

Laban asked for favor from Jacob, who wanted to leave Laban's employment after years of helping him, Laban, prosper. "Please stay, *if I have found favor in your eyes*, for I have learned by experience that the Lord has blessed me for your sake.... Name your wages, and I will give it." Jacob was favored, and this caused rich blessings in his life, but also in those with whom he associated. Favor on one invariably results in favor upon others. (Gen 30:27)

Nehemiah, cupbearer to King Nebechenezzar, grieved when he heard the wall of Jerusalem lay in ruin. Four months later, after seeking God, he asked the king, "If it pleases the king, and *if your servant has found favor in your sight*, I ask that you send me to Judah, to the city of my fathers' tombs, that I may rebuild it." Favor was granted, not just so Nehemiah could leave his employment and go to Jerusalem (no small thing, considering how dependent the king was on him!), but everything he needed to make the trip successful was also granted. Nehemiah says, "And the king granted them to me, according to the good hand of my God upon me." (Neh 2: 8) Read the book of Nehemiah some time. It is a brilliant account of a dedicated and wise man confidently flowing in the favor of God. One of my favorites.

And then, there's Esther. Oh my, the incidents of favor and the results there from are too many to cite here. If you read it, ask the Lord to open your eyes to the marvelous working of favor here. I often springboard off this text when I speak at women's retreats. Very uplifting!

(In the *Resource section* of my website, I have listed many other scriptures that talk about favor. Check them out and use them to increase your confidence that favor is God's intention for us all.)

FAVOR IS NOT JUST FOR OLD TESTAMENT SAINTS!

In the New Testament, favor and grace are often used interchangeably, but it always means an extension of something good, acceptable and of benefit to the believer.

One of the really cool definitions of favor is *"**the divine influence in our hearts, and the reflection of such in our lives.**"* It is a beneficial and significant gift, a highly elevated position, or special access or appointment.

FAVOR GIVES US A REASON TO NOT FEAR.

When the angel Gabriel came to Mary, he greeted her by saying, "Hail, Mary**, *highly favored one***. The Lord is with you!"

Did you know that ***hail*** means - be full of cheer, be happy, and be well? Happy news is coming for Mary, the first of which is she is highly favored and God is with her!

But Mary is not happy or full of cheer. She is greatly disturbed!

Sometimes encounters with God are disturbing, especially when we don't know why we are having it, or what's going on!

Nevertheless, the angel quickly reassures her and tells her to not fear…. Why? Again he says, she had found **favor with God and He was with her.** It was after that calming, yet encouraging preface that the angel gives her the good news: she will bear the Son of God. Though this would cause Mary to experience some tough times, she in all humility and gratitude accepted this as favor. (Lk. 1: 28-30)

WE NEED TO INCREASE IN FAVOR

In another example, Jesus is approaching his teens. Here the word says "He grew in stature and wisdom, and **favor with God and man.**" In this verse, favor refers to that *divine influence upon the heart and the reflection thereof in a life.* Jesus relied on the Father, and it is often said that He only did what he saw the Father do, that it was His voice to which Jesus responded. But He would also need God influencing the hearts and minds of men in order for Jesus to fulfill His mission. Hmmm… If Jesus needed to increase in favor, how about me?

WE ARE RECEIVED IN
AND RESTORED TO FAVOR

2 Cor. 5:18-20 (AMP) tells us that all things are from God, that He has received us into favor and brought us into harmony with Himself, through Christ. This is what it means to be reconciled to Him. **We have been received and restored into favor.** Done deal, my friends! The word says it is true. Indeed, Paul begs us in this passage to grab a hold of this divine favor for ourselves.

We can't earn favor or manipulate God into giving it to us. All we need to do is accept, grow in it, and use it for our benefit and the benefit of others, enjoying it as we do!

God is blessed when we receive His favor, but He is also blessed when we pass it on, teach others about it, and become favor brokers, ambassadors of reconciliation.

A HIGHER VIEW OF ACCEPTANCE

Being accepted by God is a quality of His love that we all desire. But it is fairly common for us to think that His acceptance means that no matter how flawed and imperfect I am, He will always love and accept me. That brings us a sense of relief: "At least God won't disregard me because of my flaws."

Now there is nothing wrong with this thinking, except it may cause us to be grateful to God for something that doesn't accurately reflect His heart. It's like He is saying, "Here I am, the magnificent One, putting up with these troublesome earthlings because I love them, and that's what love does." Such thinking almost imposes a reluctance upon God and a guilt upon us.

I believe there is a higher, more accurate view of being "accepted" by God.

Eph 1:6 says, we are **"accepted in the Beloved."** (KJV) This is fascinating because the Greek word used for "accepted" in this context is "charitoo," which means:

- to <u>make</u> special
- be <u>highly</u> favored
- endowed and transfused with <u>special honor</u>
- to honor with blessings
- to make graceful, charming, lovely, and agreeable

So, it's clear: your beloved God has made you special. You are highly favored, endowed with special honor, blessed, and made graceful, charming, lovely, and agreeable! This is how He sees you! This is who you are.

Does this not astound and delight you? Can you receive that as a little child and accept it as yours? That is how you increase in it! Take some time to focus on this astounding truth about you, and let it expand!

Now watch this…. The Greek word, "charitoo", in Eph. 1:6 is the same Greek word used in Lk. 1:30 when the angel tells Mary that she is *highly favored*. These are the only two times this word is used in the NT – one referring to us and the other Mary.

Yes, I know, maybe we can accept *Mary* as being highly favored, honored with blessings, and made special. After all, God picked her out and made her the mother of His Son!

But me? You?

Ephesians 1:6 says, "Yes… you!" **This is what the Almighty thinks of you!**

Let that explode in your heart and mind!

Imagine yourself wearing favor and honor, having it course through your veins, and carrying it wherever you go. I know the idea of God honoring you may be something you buck at, but it's in the Word! Not to make you feel puffed up apart from God, but grateful and receiving! Carry that thought around with you for a while, and tell me if you don't feel different about yourself!

God has made you special! Try saying these words, "God has made me special. I am His favorite." Doesn't it bring a smile to your face?

Write to the Lord. Tell Him how being His favorite makes you feel. Write down any resistance that pops up.

_____

_____

_____

_____

How do you think feeling highly favored and esteemed by God Himself would change your life?

_____

_____

_____

_____

5

STORIES OF FAVOR IN OPERATION

Oh, yes! You are special, highly favored, and given every spiritual blessing. But not just spiritual! 2 Peter 1: 3 says God has given us everything for life and godliness. Everything we need and everything over and above what we need to live a fabulous life of abundance.

Favor is God's idea, and that is such a good thing. And as we saw, His favor can influence the hearts and minds of even kings, kings who don't even believe in Him! (Remember Nebechednezzar and Nehemiah?)

Are you beginning to not just know you are God's favorite, special in every way to Him, but even more, feel it?

To further raise your consciousness of favor, I want to share a few personal stories of favor with you. As you read these, may your mind be quickened to your own stories of favor and the way it benefited your life or the lives of others.

FAVOR ON A JOB INTERVIEW

When the Lord was first opening my eyes to favor, I had an unusual thing happen. My youngest daughter, Rachel, 18 at the time, had applied for a job with a popular bank in our area. When she didn't get an invitation for an interview after a few weeks, I was reminded that my niece worked there. I called her. It turned out my niece's office was down the hall from the woman who handled all applications. Through her research, it was discovered that they had never received Rachel's application. (word to the wise, follow up all online apps!) Per their instructions, Rachel sent the new application directly to my niece who hand-carried it to the woman in charge.

Not yet having eyes to see, I didn't think of this as favor at the time. Just a fortunate thing to have a family member available to help us out. Within a short period of time, Rachel was called for an interview.

The morning of her interview — and this is the strange part — I awoke with a vision. At the time, I was not accustomed to visions. In fact, my left brain training resisted visions, and my religious training rejected them all together. But this … I could not deny.

In the vision, Rachel was standing there in a beautiful gown. The Lord, next to her, was holding a crown over her head. From the crown, a glistening amber substance flowed and covered her from head to toe. As it did, the Lord said, "Today, it will not be your experience, clothing, or personality that they see. It will be My favor." I jumped out of bed, and excitedly shared this good news with Rachel as she was getting ready. "Cool," was her simple response.

Not long after, it struck me that I had never prepared her for an interview with a financial institution. I knew the way to dress, what to say, and how to carry yourself. But I had told her none of that.

How could I have been so derelict? Moved by guilt and apprehension, the temptation to give her a crash course in interview techniques overtook me, and just when I was about to do so, she came downstairs and said, "How do I look?"

Thankfully the horror on my face was well masked, as I noticed her blonde hair fried from too many changes in color, the glittery "diamonds" in her barrettes, way too much makeup, and finally, a pair of wrinkled pants. All I could think was.... Where do I start??

But God, lovely, amazing God, closed my mouth and reminded me of the vision. Oh, I see. That was for me! I smiled, and said, "You look wonderful. God bless you." And off she went.

She was hired.

To see the favor of God in operation, despite the absence of textbook strategies, was a major lesson for me.

ACHIEVING OUR DREAMS

In Michael Oher's life we clearly see favor as a necessary element in him **achieving his dreams**. He was in the right place at the right time crossing paths of the right people. Again, often it is diligently pursuing our dreams and getting ourselves ready that make that kind of magnetic setting highly advantageous.

Similarly, I was focused on my dream of becoming an attorney, but studying and working hard wasn't all that was necessary for my "big break." Indeed, favor was working before I even attended my first class.

It was the first week of law school. Our school's annual tennis tournament was about to begin. Sitting on the grass ready to watch the first match, I overheard this guy complaining about the absence of his tennis partner. Without even thinking, my passion for tennis spoke up and I offered to be his partner.

After testing my ability, Tom, my soon to be partner, accepted and we won. Over the year, we partnered in a number of competitions. Tom graduated, and I lost touch with him … until the spring before the end of my second year.

One day, while walking past the bulletin board outside the Placement Office, I noticed Tom's name on a little 3x5 card. Now, I want you to see something: I walk fast, I talk fast, and I am usually very focused on where I am going. Not only that, but I was not looking for work. I had a part time job, and was already chosen to be a Legal Writing and Research Teaching Assistant for third year. I was set!

But there I was, and there was his name, and it was calling to me. Curious, I stopped; read that a position as a legal intern for the State's criminal justice system had an opening. Interestingly, I had no interest in criminal law, as evidenced by my low test scores, and yet, I felt compelled to call about the position.

Tom set me up and I was granted an interview with the most powerful man in the state. I want you to notice – while my legal education was necessary to me getting the job, it was my relationship to an old tennis partner that got me in the door.

Now, I have to add something very interesting here. Years prior to this I had a group of friends who were excellent tennis players. After many balls shooting off my racket into no mans' land, my friends sort of disappeared when they made arrangements to play. I got the hint.

But I also liked tennis, despite how badly I played, and an even greater motivator… I hated being excluded because I was so bad at something.

So, I invested in private lessons with a tennis pro. Little did I know, but hidden in me was a natural talent. All I needed was someone to work with me to draw it out. Eventually I had the good pleasure of astounding my friends with my newly acquired skills!

Who would have known that a few years later tennis would also be the vehicle through which this golden opportunity with the State would come? Favor often works through our special interests.

Back to the interview. I would like to say that it went well, but it was actually horrific. Grilled and humiliated by someone who seemed like a crazed power hungry psycho, hardly seemed worth the one- hour drive. The way he treated me? No way was I getting the job. In fact, in an attempt to further intimidate me, he lit my resume on fire, smirking as he watched it burn, just to demonstrate his poor opinion of it and his power over me.

I nervously laughed at the absurdity of this act and was thus, immediately expelled from his office. Stunned, I exited, leaned against the wall outside his door, completely aghast at what just happened. Then I did what no woman who is climbing the ladder to success should do… I cried like a little girl.

I've often wondered if this was part of the whole mind game thing, but within seconds, Tom came along, saw me whimpering pathetically, and stormed into the boss's office. After a bit of indiscernible yelling, I was called back in and informed that I had the job. WHAT?!

Well, despite this dreadful beginning, securing this position was an amazing work of favor. After interning, they asked me to stay on and after passing the Bar, I became a full-fledged prosecutor, met some of the most intriguing people of my life, made incredible friends, and resolved some major confidence issues.

MY CHILDREN

Whether adopted, biologically born, or step-parenting, raising children is a special privilege. But I did not always think so. As a career woman, I had little interest in having babies. I did not have that biological time clock that women always talk about, ticking away, waiting for the day I would be a mom. In fact, I couldn't even see myself as a mom … ever.

But that wasn't God's plan.

I met my husband, fell in love, and along with him came the most beautiful and captivating children I had ever met, Rebecca and Eric. It was love at first sight. Gene and I were married and I became a mom. I will never forget when Eric, at 11 or 12, instructing me in what moms are supposed to carry in their purse for their kids. I was most appreciative for the lesson.

Because of my love for my new kids, and all that they were going through, Gene and I agreed that we need not have any children of our own, and with Gene having had a vasectomy previously, this worked for him too. We were more than satisfied with that decision.

But God had other ideas.

When Gene and I married, we decided to dedicate our marriage and our lives to the Lord. Whatever He wanted us to do, wherever He wanted us to go, whenever he wanted it to happen — we were committed to Him first.

The aspect of favor, the ***divine influence on our hearts and the reflection of such in a life,*** occurred frequently as we continually opened ourselves up to God's transforming mind-renewal program.

I began to be divinely influenced about children. Something strange began to happen to me. I found myself mysteriously lingering over babies. Alarmed at this strange sensation, I kept it to myself, remembering my agreement.

Unbeknownst to me, Gene was also being "divinely influenced," on his drives home from work, listening to a popular speaker talk about the value of children. Gene was crazy about his kids, but this radio program gave him an even greater appreciation for them. Additionally, God stunningly moved in his heart to tell me that I needed to have a child from birth, not just inherit them as teenagers.

I cried. The idea of me having a baby and maybe actually being good at it was overwhelming. We moved forward in excitement.

Reversals were pretty common, we discovered, and the chances of success were good. Insurance was approved and the date was set. One day before the surgery, however, the insurance company reneged. We would have to save up to have it done. We decided to do so. Good plan, but God's was better.

About a week later, I ran into an old friend at a bible study. I was quite amazed that she had twin babies. Why, I didn't even know she was pregnant! To my surprise, she was adopting these little gems! I had never known anyone who adopted, but seeing my curiosity, she asked if I was interested in adoption because she knew a young mom who was looking for a qualified couple.

Me? Adopt? As soon as I could, I called Gene to see if he would even consider it. And of course he did! Whatever God wanted, Gene wanted. So, we took one scary step at a time, and in a few weeks we met the birthmother. Beautiful and barely sixteen, she greeted us at the door of a mutual acquaintance. It was instant love. Within minutes of discussion, she excused herself to tell the agency and five other families that she had found her couple. Immense favor surrounded us all. I trust the people who were waiting found the baby that was meant for them, but thankfully, Rachel was meant for us.

Within three months of that first conversation, we had our little darling, and life has never been the same.

God knew what was best for all of us. When we were disqualified for the reversal, we felt disappointed for sure, but not hopeless. We still had plenty of time. But God had a better way. And His favor set the whole thing up, right down to moving in someone's heart to pay for the whole thing! We just followed His lead, trusting Him with the outcome. I'm so glad I didn't try and control that one!

FAVOR TO IMPACT THE LIFE OF ANOTHER
When Rachel was two, we decided it was time to pursue adoption again.

Early in the process we received a windfall check for over $2000. I thought it was for the adoption of our new baby, whenever that was to happen. But my husband had a feeling, as did a friend that the money was not for us, but for a birth mother. What? I vehemently opposed this idea.

Soon after, we were once again chosen by a birth mother, who we invited to come and live with us the month before the baby was born. I would pick her up at the airport, be the labor coach, and take care of her through the delivery, at which point, she would return to her home state.

As planned, I picked her up at the airport, and like with Rachel's birth-mom, I instantly fell in love with her. Wow! Another quick and easy adoption! So far, so good!

But then, all of a sudden, as I was putting her luggage into the trunk, "divine influence" came upon my heart like a thunderbolt, and with unspeakable joy, I asked her if we helped her, would she like to keep her baby. She cried and said yes. So, as it turned out, the $2000 was meant for her after all. I felt absolutely no sense of loss, but thoroughly enthused about the role we would play in her life. It was favor from God, through us, to her. It was amazing!

After our counsel and assistance, that woman ended up marrying the father of her child. Later he completed his PhD., and she her Master's degree, and they had two more beautiful children. Twenty-one years later, they are still married.

FAVOR TO PROTECT

Over the next six months, the baby project was quiet. No calls. No interest. No nothing … until we were connected to another birth mom. We were called when she went into delivery, drove to the hospital with great anticipation and excitement, only to discover the baby had died from lack of prenatal care. Because I was the prospective mother, her family asked that I attend the baby's funeral. I was completely stunned and angry that this could happen, and thus, after the death, withdrew from the world.

Six months later, with my hope renewed, we began to get called for interviews. Several near matches later, and more heartbreaking no's, I was once again done. Then our counselor begged for one more interview.

This was the jackpot … our Joe. However, there would be a delay, a change of mind, and then when he was three months old, the demand for him back.

This was my son. And though we loved this young couple who gave us a blessing of immeasurable worth, they at the time, were violent and incapable of caring for themselves, much less, him. But we had no legal recourse. We had to give him back. Fear for his safety consumed my heart.

After processing this terrifying reality, and getting people to pray nationwide, God reassured my heart. Not that He would make sure Joe stayed with us, but He had His eye on him and no matter what, He would keep him safe. With that revelation and reassurance, we met with the couple. Maybe we could talk some sense into them. Maybe we could work something out.

God had it all under control. Over the next two days, He intervened and came to both of them individually, and made His will known. In "divine influence," the power of God moved in their minds and hearts, and Joe became ours for good.

God's favor has been on Joe since the beginning of time, and God knew that Joe would need this dramatic story to quell any of his doubts regarding his value and worth. I am grateful.

As you can see, the favor of God and man has been critical to the very formation of our family, the fulfillment of our goals, and the means to helping others. It's a powerful thing!

FAVOR TO HEAL

Wouldn't you agree that being healed of a debilitating, painful condition is a huge favor?

A number of years ago, I learned I had a rare, incurable, untreatable, eye disease. The prognosis was scary: ultimate and complete blindness. Blindness was probably the thing I feared most in life. Maybe it was due to my study of Helen Keller and Louis Braille in 6th grade, I don't know, but I could not have received worse news.

Being strong, healthy, and active all my life, I had not paid much attention to God's will on healing. I was woefully ignorant on the subject. I panicked.

Little by little things came into our path: people, studies, and ministries. We would soon realize that we needed a major overhaul in our belief system. The belief system I had, produced nothing but fear.

This fear manifested in horrendous migraines that would last for days, put me out of commission, and sometimes into the hospital. Knowing it may be stress did not help to stop them. In fact, it exacerbated them because I also felt guilty being a counselor that had so much fear. In other words, I knew better.

In addition to the migraines, I had a myriad of other conditions: painful fibroid cysts, gall bladder pain, stomach problems, and even occasional anxiety attacks, where I was sure I was dying.

Because I was advancing in age, I wondered if this was just the normal downhill slide so many seniors talk about. "Is this what I have to look forward to? Going from one bad condition to the next?"

I was not happy.

One morning after several days of incapacitation from a migraine, lying in my bed, crying from pain, a thought interrupted my plight: "Call someone to pray who will stay until the headache is gone." Oddly enough, I knew exactly who to call. Without hesitating, my friend Suzanne, who was a new student herself when it came to healing, dropped everything and attended to me. What a magnificent gesture of favor!

Despite a few confusing, and now comical moments, Suzanne tapped into the love of God for me, spoke it out, and I was instantly, totally, and forever healed. I never got another migraine. For those of you migraine sufferers, you know what kind of relief I'm talking about. (Thank you, Lord.)

The favor was not just the healing, the leading, and the teaching. His favor also uncovered a well hidden, totally subconscious belief I was not even aware of: "Does God love me enough to heal me?" Often I had languished on my bed feeling quite abandoned, wondering where God was and how He could let me lay there in so much pain.

Whether He was waiting for the right time, right person, and/or the right place … I don't know. All I know is that everything lined up correctly and God healed me — in my body and my mind, forever.

EMOTIONS AND THE HUMAN BODY

Though this is not a story, I wanted to add this additional piece. How we feel about ourselves and the issues of life have clinically proven consequences in our bodies, and ultimately our health. There is no dispute that prolonged stress and negative emotions damage our cardiovascular systems. Cardiovascular disease is still the leading cause of death in America. Diet is partly responsible, but even more significant is attitude and approach to life. (I dare say, even diet is heavily connected to our emotions and how we process life!)

The good news is - positive emotions, which include feeling special, can actually undo cardiovascular effects caused by negative emotions. This is just one of many powerful effects positive emotions have on our bodies.

You have your own stories. Imagine it! Write it! Share it!

6

THE POWER OF APPROVAL

One of the most invigorating and comforting experiences we can have is feeling the approval of someone that matters to us. God put this need for approval within us, and it is He who has the ability to fulfill it! ***Inherent in favor is approval.***

- Do you feel approved of by God?
- Do you believe you must earn God's approval?
- Do you wonder if God is disappointed with or in you?

How you answer these questions will affect the freedom you have in approaching God and the security you have in having your prayers answered.

In Luke 3:21-22, Jesus was about to embark on His ministry and was baptized by John the Baptist. After such, He prayed and "heaven was opened.[22] And the Holy Spirit descended in bodily form like a dove upon Him, and a voice came from heaven which said, "You are My beloved Son; in You I am well pleased."

Notice, Jesus had not done anything yet! No healing, no teachings, no deliverances. Nevertheless, the Father declared His approval. This is His favor on His Son.

Do you fully comprehend that you, too, have the Father's favor?

I believe the Father's approval is vital for the work we do, but the basis for it is *our relationship, not our performance.* We do not need to strive for His pleasure! If we understand we already have it, and work from that place of security and significance, we will not approach our work with the added burden of trying to measure up or prove ourselves.

Instead, work becomes a way to reveal our already existing power and worth, and a means to bless the world around us with it.

Charles M. Schwab, founder of Bethlehem Steel, once said, " I have yet to find a man, however exalted his station, who did not do ***better work and put forth greater effort*** under a ***spirit of approval*** than under a ***spirit of criticism***."

Brilliant.

Do you feel approved by God, merely because you are His? Or are you still stuck in the cycle of performance, desperately trying to earn His blessings and favor?

Do you treat others with favor because of your relationship with them, or only when they do a "good enough" job, or have something you want?

Consider the Father's way, and extend favor to those with whom you are in relationship. It will bless both your hearts.

Favor represents the true heart of God to a world that desperately needs Him. It can begin with you.

There is a work of God with which I am thoroughly impressed: *Iris Ministries*, founded by Heidi and Rolland Baker. It is a healing, providing, and loving arm of God to the people, especially the children of Mozambique.

Besides setting up orphanages, feeding the hungry, healing the blind, deaf, dumb, and crippled, the Bakers work tirelessly, but in absolute joy, loving these people. The obstacles they meet can't even be imagined, and yet they are one of the most productive Kingdom ministries on this planet.

I wondered before the Lord how they have been able to accomplish such a great work. He highlighted this:

> *"Our total trust in our Savior is the substance of our intimacy with Him, and* ***no self-condemnation or weakness*** *can diminish our fiery love affair with our God.*
>
> *We trust Jesus to save us from ourselves. We trust Him to take initiative in and through us. All bright ideas come from Him, and He has no lack of them! We are set completely free from all pressure. There is no compulsion in His Kingdom.*
>
> ***....In Jesus we are the crowning achievement of all His creative power...*** *We and our lives are the field of the activity of His mind, which we must never underestimate. We are the outcome and substance of His joy. By His Spirit we partake of His pleasure, taking the perfection of relationship that could rise only from His infinite imagination. He delights in His own handiwork, which is our delight in Him. How perfect is our God!*
>
> *...By taking pleasure in our God, we rout the enemy. By pursuing the free gift of holiness and* ***refusing condemnation***, *we find every reason to be lighthearted."* [15]

It is clear from the Bakers' example that the "joy of the Lord" is their strength. It is also clear that their joy is closely connected to their refusal to feel any sense of condemnation, though they often are the object of it. Most of us know that "there is no condemnation in Jesus," but what do we do instead?

The Bakers tell us what they do instead… believe, agree, and receive that they are the **"crowning achievement of all His creative power."** But not just they, but all of mankind. This is the heart from which they serve the broken and powerless. They see this high value in everyone, and people come flocking to them daily.

Do you think the Bakers feel such approval **because** of their work, or is the success of their work and the joy in their hearts greater because they are **confident** that they **are approved by God**?

I encourage you to develop your trust in Him and His view of you. He desires to increase your concept of favor, and show you, that you too, are **"the crowning achievement of all His creative expression."**

Pray out loud: Thank you Lord, that I too, am the crowning achievement of all Your creative expression! May I view the rest of the world with those eyes! Give me eyes to see!

Write your thoughts as you said this:

_____

_____

_____

_____

7

FAVOR AND FAITH
WORK HAND IN HAND

Favor is instrumental in the fulfillment our dreams, having a quality life, and positively impacting the world. And faith activates it.

Just ask Susan Boyle. Singing since age 12, mostly in church and around town, at 47, she took the plunge and auditioned in 2009 on *Britain's Got Talent.*

(If you have not seen the video, please, stop right now and go to YouTube.com and take a look. I never get tired of watching it. I cry every time. You'll have no trouble finding it.)

When Susan entered the stage, hand on one hip, her confident cheekiness seemed to be an insulating force against the multitude of mockery. Even Simon's eye-rolls didn't seem to dissuade her.

Like many, I was as stunned as the judges as soon as she sang her first note. I am not proud to say that I, too, judged a book by its cover, and expected something far different than Susan delivered. It was a lesson for us all.

Whatever Susan thought about her own outward appearance, it was irrelevant to her as she pursued her dream, and with sweet clarity and an unparalleled demonstration of soul, she moved us in the depths of our hearts with her brilliant version of "I Dreamed a Dream".

Like many others, I have been compelled to learn as much as I could about Susan. Suffering more than her share of bullying and mistreatment, it would be natural and understandable for Susan to lose sight of her dream, or even dare to dream at all.

But that's not all.

Prior to Susan's big break, she was alone, having lost her mother who she lived with her whole life, was unemployed, and never married. What must she have been thinking?

Maybe these words of the song she sang reflect what she and many of us who have had dreams have felt:

I DREAMED A DREAM
There was a time when men were kind
When their voices were soft
And their words inviting
There was a time when love was blind
And the world was a song
And the song was exciting

There was a time
Then it all went wrong

I dreamed a dream in time gone by
When hope was high
And life worth living
I dreamed that love would never die
I dreamed that God would be forgiving
Then I was young and unafraid
And dreams were made and used and wasted
There was no ransom to be paid
No song unsung, no wine untasted

But the tigers come at night
With their voices soft as thunder
As they tear your hope apart
And they turn your dream to shame

He slept a summer by my side
He filled my days with endless wonder
He took my childhood in his stride
But he was gone when autumn came

And still I dream he'll come to me
That we will live the years together
But there are dreams that cannot be
And there are storms we cannot weather

I had a dream my life would be
So different from this hell I'm living
So different now from what it seemed
Now life has killed the dream I dreamed.[16]

And yet…. Life did not kill Susan's dream. Maybe there were times it felt like it was dying, or she questioned if it would ever be fulfilled, or if it was even worth it all. But her dream never died.

How often I talk to people who no longer have a dream. It's been snuffed out, forgotten, or replaced by cynicism. But once they are poked and prodded a bit, something rises…. Hope and faith.

And that is exactly what sustained Susan. She could have crawled under a rock with that glorious voice of hers, like many do, but she had something better than gold, and that was her faith.

In an interview with *Christianity Today*, Susan said, "You're looking at someone who would get the belt every day. 'Will you Shut up, Susan!' - whack! …. I'm just a wee bit slower at picking things up than other people. So you get left behind in a system that just wants to rush on, you know? That was what I felt was happening to me."

In another interview Susan recounts it was her looks, especially her "frizzy" hair, which was the object of ridicule.

Indeed, this is not the fertile ground for success one would think!

But then Susan explains the real foundation for her overcoming all obstacles, *"I have my faith, which is the backbone of who I am, really."* *(CT, Brain Hutt, 11/17/2009)*

There will always be those around who will try to convince us that we are nothing, have nothing to offer, and should expect nothing. But that is not God's view of us. Knowing what He thinks and accepting it as true for ourselves is a major first step in living the life He designed for us.

Susan Boyle, though at 47 had never been married or even kissed, obviously did not believe she was a nothing, or meant for nothing.

Behind the scenes of the talent show, she said with a "nothing is going to stop me" glint in her eyes, "I always wanted to perform before a large audience. I'm going to make that audience rock!"

They did not just rock; they were mesmerized. They were undone, and rose to their feet in a standing ovation to show her just how proud they were of her.

Read the words of the song she is singing now:

WHO I WAS BORN TO BE
When I was a child
I could see the wind in the trees
And I heard a song in the breeze
It was there, singing out my name

But I am not a girl
I have known the taste of defeat
And I have finally grown to believe
It will all came around again

And though I may not
Know the answers
I can finally say I am free
And if the questions
Led me here, then
I am who I was born to be
And so here am I
Open arms and ready to stand
I've got the world in my hands
And it feels like my turn to fly

When I was a child
There were flowers that bloomed in the night
Unafraid to take in the light
Unashamed to have braved the dark

I am who I was born to be
I am who I was born to be.[17]

Susan is living her life's purpose. She is taking this magnificent gift, sharing it with the world, and through it and her story, we are encouraged, inspired, and hopefully, our own God-given dreams are resurrected.

But there's even more to this story…

James Martin, S.J. from *American Magazine* says it well:

"The way we see Susan Boyle is very nearly the way God sees us: worthwhile, special, talented, unique, beautiful. The world generally looks askance at people like Susan Boyle, if it sees them at all. Without classic good looks, without work, without a spouse, living in a small town, people like Susan Boyle may not seem particularly "important." But God sees the real person, and understands the value of each individual's gifts: rich or poor, young or old, single or married, matron or movie star, lucky or unlucky in life. God knows us — and He loves us.

'**Everybody is somebody**' said Archbishop Timothy M. Dolan at his installation Mass in New York City yesterday. That's another reason why the judges smile and the audience explodes in applause.

Because they recognized a basic truth planted deep within them by God: **Susan Boyle is somebody. Everybody is somebody.**"[18]

Well said, Mr. Martin.

We don't have to succumb to the negativity of our past, or even the hardships of today.

There is a voice within, maybe a quiet one right now, but it's there — and it says, "You were made for more. You are loved and will overcome this."

I am absolutely convinced that those thoughts are God's thoughts, put in the spirit of man.

Did you know the Word is replete with passages that show that God wants us to be successful? He wants us to triumph over our circumstances. That is why we all love a good hero story. True accounts of down and outers overcoming all odds and conquering their fears, circumstances or obstacles will never go out of style. They inspire our hearts.

Why this universal reaction?

Because we are made in the image of God. We are His creation, and He put that spirit of victory in our hearts. It is His voice within that reminds us of who we are and for what we are created.

Embracing God's favorable view of us, even when no one else does, takes faith, childlike faith. But doing so will give you the heart as well as the ability to overcome obstacles, negative feedback, and disheartening discouragement.

Take inventory of your gifts and talents. Develop them, and while doing so, accept God's favor. Be confident that they have been given to you for His pleasure, your pleasure, and to benefit the world.

What do you do well?

_____

_____

_____

What do you love to do?

_____

_____

What is so easy for you that it frustrates you that other people can't do it?

_____

_____

_____

What obstacles do you face?

_____

_____

_____

Have they caused you to want to give up?

_____

_____

_____

In the next chapter, we will take a look at some effective ways to increase your faith and favor.

8

LET GOD CONVINCE YOU

By this point in the book, hopefully your consciousness has already been raised. That's good! We can learn so much about what God desires for us by reading other people's stories. And yet, until we see we have our own, we are not convinced.

God wants you convinced. Doubt makes us double minded, which makes us confused, unstable, and ineffective. The Spirit of God is not a spirit of fear, but of power, love, and a sound mind. A sound mind is a stable mind, a wise mind, and **mind which agrees with God.**

He says over and over in His Word that you have His favor, His approval, His acceptance, His esteem and honor. May His Spirit of truth flow freely into your mind and renew it!

If you are still here with me, then most likely God has made favor important to you, personally, like He did with me. I have no doubt He will show you the way, but here are some tips that have been instrumental to me being convinced.

1. WORSHIP

Since volumes could be written on worship alone, and I am just a worshipper, not an expert, I will only share what it means to me. I believe we are created to worship. It is one of the most effective means I know to transport me out of the doldrums, clear up confusion, and set me straight.

In worship, the Lord and I immediately connect. I feel at one with my Friend, my King, my Master, my Creator. My whole perspective shifts for the better. I feel elevated, renewed, and at peace. I dance, breathe, and enjoy Him as He enjoys me. I experience His favor in worship.

Mostly I worship with music. I have a number of songs, readily available to me that, upon hearing them, my heart immediately swells and I smile.

A caveat here ... Sometimes worship can seem like something you only do in church, or maybe the songs you are familiar with have become rote, or lifeless, or not your taste. May I suggest you take some time to listen to a variety of music and put together a CD or save on your computer worship songs that opens your heart to hear and feel His heartbeat. Worship is definitely for anywhere and anytime, by whatever means you can connect with God intimately.

Also, I realize that worship can also be in things we do. In this discussion, I am focusing on worship as a means of connecting with God so we become more convinced of His love and favor for us.

Worship, for me, is simply pouring out my love to the Lord and receiving His love back. During worship I feel free to abandon myself to Him, fully trusting in His loving kindness, mercy, and power in and through me.

I know of no other way to more quickly come into awareness of His favor.

2. KNOW HIM

If God is the Source of a love that we all desperately crave, and favor is a by-product of that love, then knowing Him intimately, experientially, and correctly just seems to make sense! **Knowing God is knowing love.**

2 Peter 2: 1 says, *"Grace and peace be multiplied to you in the knowledge of God and Jesus our Lord."*

This is not just a perfunctory greeting. This is a power packed principle. Let's look a little more closely.

From my resource, grace is used over 130 times in the New Testament alone. And in this verse, it means graciousness, favor, the divine influence on the heart, acceptability, benefit and pleasure. Don't you want that?

And peace? Prosperity, oneness, rest ... Wouldn't you like that also?

But Peter does not offer just a little of it. No, he says, may it be **multiplied.** Here it means increase and abound.

To who? To you.

How? In the knowledge of God and Jesus our Lord.

What kind of knowledge? Intimate, deep, fully acquainted knowledge. The kind of knowledge you have with your dearest friends, your husband, or your children. And dare I say, even deeper than that?

My husband is my best friend on this whole planet. We are privileged to be able to both work at home, which affords us the ability to have lots of time to talk, share, and relax together. It's lovely. And as well as I know him and as much as we share, I do believe I know God better. Why? Because He is IN me.

How do you get to know Him so intimately?

I am assuming that if you are reading this you already have a personal relationship with God, through Jesus, but maybe you are just not feeling the love. Most everyone who decides to counsel with me seems to be in that condition. Knowing He loves you and experiencing His love can be worlds apart sometimes.

So, besides worship, what do I suggest?

- **Interact with Him**

Well, I don't suggest what people call "devotions," if they are ritualistic and just a duty to check off.

Several months ago I attended a conference where Wm. Paul Young, author of *The Shack*, spoke. In one of his sessions, he shared how he did not have personal "devotions." It was like he lobbed a bomb on the religious mind. How could he "dis" one of the primary spiritual disciplines and evidences of a godly life? Harummph!

And yet, it is clear that having morning "devotions," has become more like a legalistic bondage from which we need to be delivered, rather than heart to heart encounters we yearn for with our Lord.

Whenever a teacher or preacher talks about spending time with the Lord, the common response is a guilty, "I know I should, but..." and off the person goes to the flogging room in the dark recesses of their mind.

If this is you, let me reassure you: **Feeling guilty will actually hinder you from experiencing Him and His favor.** So, decide now that you will not succumb to a spirit of criticism or condemnation. You are free to be with God, hear His voice, and feel His pleasure … at any time, anywhere!

In the *Resource* section of my website there are some wonderful resources to help you know the voice of God and hear Him while driving, working, or on a lunch break. One favorite place for many is… the shower!

Having said all that, I must tell you, I do meet with my Friend and my King in the mornings before my mind gets so cluttered with the tasks of the day. I call this my *"Java, Jammies, and Jesus"* time, and I love it. The Lord so fills my imagination with thoughts of Him, me, and life in general, that it is like play time to me.

This is indeed a favor to me of the highest regard.

- **Learn how to hear His voice**

Several years ago, I was challenged by the realization that I didn't really know how to hear the voice of God. Though I had been a teacher and biblical counselor, with my own daily study time, hearing, seeing, or even feeling God directly was rare.

True to form, God took my stirred up spirit and placed in my path several excellent teachings to guide me. Through them I learned that hearing His voice is not as mystical as it seems. It's actually quite easy to do, mainly because He says, "My sheep hear My voice." With His Spirit in us, we are meant to hear His voice! If you are insecure about this as I was, get a hold of some of the resources listed, but I can also help you personally.

You can become confident in hearing His voice without a lot of striving. He is on your side.

- **Write to Him**

Now this may sound a little weird to some of you. Some of you may not be writers. But if you text message or send emails, you can write to God. I write to Him almost daily.

Ever **write to a friend** who lives in another part of the country? Does writing to her make you feel connected? Do you imagine being with her as you write? Do you share secrets or intimacies? You can do the same with God. I have come to realize that it delights His heart!

How about a **thank you note**? Not one of those your mother made you write to be polite, but a genuine heartfelt thank you. Express why you are thankful, what you liked, and how it blessed you. You could do this every day and never run out of things to say. There is always so much to be thankful for, and the more we are aware of the blessings in our lives, the more they grow!

Letters of complaints are also welcomed. Just look at how David often went on and on and on. Sometimes this mighty king was a big 'ole cry baby. But in his letters, the Psalms, he always comes back to the truth. "God is mighty, all good, and loves me. He is always actively working in my life, even when I am not aware." Though we do not want to live negativity, and continually speak words of death over our lives, we need to know that we can go to our God, who cares, and download our troubles, and be assured He will help us.

These are just a few suggestions. Besides drawing you closer to God, letters also keep you on track. Many times people tell me that they don't know what to do when they meet with God, or their mind just wanders all over the place. They feel that time has been wasted, and so they are not encouraged to come back.

Once they see the amazing results of writing to Him, invariably they are back for more. Thoughts from deep within, ones that they were not even conscious of, come flooding to the forefront. Together with the Lord, they can be dealt with.

• **Other considerations**

In helping people I have become convinced that the lack of time to meet with the Lord is rarely the real culprit. It's actually doubt or fear. Doubt that the time taken will actually prove to be well spent, or fear of what God might say.

While I can't cover this topic in any length here, here's a few questions that may tell you if this is a problem for you:

- Has previous attempts to spend time in the Word or with Him been unfruitful?
- Do you sometimes show up, Bible in hand, and ask dumbfounded, "Now what?"
- Does your mind drift off or get overcrowded with chores for the day?
- Do you fear what He may say to you?
- Do you wonder if God is disappointed, irritated, or frustrated with you?
- Are you afraid He will order you to a life of poverty, in a mud hut in the depths of the jungle, eating mealy worms to prove you love Him?
- Do you have a family member you are angry with and you are

worried that God will tell you to forgive them?

Yes to any of these questions will cause a subconscious avoidance.

I suggest you write to the Lord, and tell him your concern. Then listen to what word of life and love He has for you. He is faithful.

- **Ask for eyes to see (knowing Him)**

Seeing is key to experiencing.

Have you seen the movie *Avatar*? A masterpiece in computer graphic imaging, it also illustrated some pretty provocative spiritual analogies. Christian or not, movies that portray a universality for our need for God and the spiritual is useful to me.

In the movie, a phrase often used is, "I see you." Clearly those who have humble, open hearts can see things those who know-it-all cannot. Jake Sully, an ex-Marine, recomposed as an Avatar exploring Pandora and the Navi's, is saved by Neytiri, the clan princess, from being destroyed by some pretty nasty looking beasts. After chewing him out, she explains that she saved him because she could see that he was pure.

Seeing the essence of someone is a gift.

I think we have that gift. While it is often blocked and obscured by our fears and prejudices, being at one with God, we have the capacity to see.

Again, Jesus says we are to see and understand as little children, not older children or teenaged children. By the time one gets to those later years of child development, our vision is beginning to get tainted, right?

So, how do we see clearly who God is and who we are, especially with all the specks of dirt in our eyes?

... *Simply Ask.*

Now, this was mentioned in a prior chapter, but here I want to zero in on the conscious act of asking. So, now, ask God to open your eyes, your ears, and your heart to see His favorable view of you, and the favor He offers in, around, and through you.

My prayer for you is the same as Paul's in Eph 1:18 – that the eyes of your heart would be flooded with light, focused and clear, so you can know and perceive God deeply and personally, grasping the immeasurable and unlimited and surpassing greatness of His power which is in you.

You are an extravagant work of God! Embracing this truth will give you endless, boundless strength and energy!! Ask for eyes to see!

You are rooted and held securely by His love. God has designed you to know this. But He wants more for you than just knowing it. He wants you living in that reality, experiencing for yourself this profound love and favor. He wants to you to be wholly filled and flooded with His presence, fully aware of His energy and goodness toward you. He wants to connect with you and convince you.

Why? Why does He care?

Believe it or not, God wants you to feel happy! Yes, for the sake of happiness, but also, happy people are contagious!

In addition, then He will be able to carry out His beautiful purposes in you and for you, more freely, effectively, and joyfully.

As Eph 3:20 says, "He is able to do superabundantly, far over and above all that we [dare] ask or think [infinitely beyond our highest prayers, desires, thoughts, hopes, or dreams]." This is for us!

So, ask God to flood the eyes of your heart with light. Ask Him to let you see all that is good about Him and good about you.

3. USE YOUR GOD-GIVEN IMAGINATION – VISUALIZING

Visualization is a powerful tool given to us by God. Casting vision, seeing a work of art in our mind before it is created, recalling a wonderful place we visited .... These are all done in our imaginations. That God would visit us there is not so strange.

The first time I attempted to visualize Jesus and I together, I was very leery. Having been an attorney and developing the left part of my brain, using my imagination (a primarily right brain activity) — or at least being aware of using it — was not easy for me. Once a friend invited me to attend a class to learn how to visualize and I turned her down. Besides my perceived difficulty, it did not seem like something a Christian should do. Thankfully God has corrected my thinking on that!

I will never forget the very first experience I had where God met me in my imagination. Since I didn't know how to do this, I simply prayed, and asked for Him to come, and bam!

There we were together… under an apple tree in the middle of a park! Immediately I saw the look of sheer delight and appreciation in His eyes for me… for me? Oh, no doubt about it. For me.

I then asked Him a question. He took my hands and calmly, clearly answered. It didn't really address my question, and yet, my heart was totally settled.

I have had many apple tree visitations, and I have learned that those were times when I needed reassurance and security, times when knowing He is pleased with me was all I needed.

Other times we would walk, particularly along a sea. He would put His arm around me and then stop and turn me toward the water. We would stare in silence. Once He said to me, "do you see that expanse? That is smaller than what I have in store for you. My love, My opportunities, My power are vast. They are for you. " Oh my.

And on another occasion, I met the Lord in the woods. We walked through until we came to a little house in the clearing. We went inside and there was a blazing fire in the fire place. Two couches flanked the fireplace on both sides. We each took one.

After staring at the flickering lights for a bit, I knew there was something more than staring at flames going on, as lovely as that was. Knowing what I was thinking, the Lord got up, extended His hand and led me out the back door. It was a lovely yard, and as we walked a few feet, I saw a sudden drop off. Bringing me to the edge, the Lord paused, giving me a chance to take in the magnificent vistas. What a view!

If that wasn't enough, He grabbed my hand, and off we went. Flying! Now I know there are plenty of you out there who have flying dreams, but I have never had these types of dreams — certainly not while I'm awake! Did you know brain scientists today have discovered that we can experience the same emotions in our imagination as we can in the physical? I have to confirm ... it is true.

But God wasn't finished. There was more to experience.

As we flew up overhead, He pointed out various houses. With something like X-ray vision, I could see who was in those houses. Instructed to go down and get them one by one, I escorted them to a field. We all assembled there, except for the Lord, who remained in the sky. With a twinkle in His eye, He called us all up. And guess what we did there? Dance.

The women He had chosen were women who had been stuck in some issues for which they needed freedom. His answer to the problems: Come out, fly, and dance with Him.

On another occasion, I was at a conference for coaches. I went to dinner with another attendant and we shared our lives. She told me that she had lived in a religious cult for nineteen years. After 19 years, she realized that she had completely lost her sense of self. The control, the manipulation and the shame laid on her if she had a thought of her own caused her to leave and seek therapy. At the point I met her, she had had therapy for twenty years at $1000/mo. I felt much compassion for her, for she still seemed tormented.

When it was my turn to share, I told her about a new course I was working on, where one of the exercises involved visualizing. I did not invite her to try it. I merely shared what the exercise entailed.

"Imagine Jesus sitting at the head of a table laden with rich delicacies, gourmet foods, and sweet drinks. It is a sight to behold. You enter the room. He has been eagerly awaiting your arrival and upon seeing you, He stands up, walks toward you, and extends His hand to you. You take it and He leads you to your chair, right next to His. The look in His eye says it all. You are His precious one."

As soon as I finished describing the scene, tears filled her eyes and she said, "I think that did more for me than twenty years of therapy." She then went on to tell me about her life growing up in a strict Christian home. She had experienced God as mean, and thus turned away from Christianity and Him.

God used this image to fill her heart with a new vision of Him. She then said, "I always thought He loved me. I always wanted Him to love me. But now I know He does." And she continued to weep as I held her in my arms. I was amazed.

Through visualizing, others and I have been able to see and experience parts of God we never knew before. Not only has He taught us about who He is and who we are to Him, but also, how He feels about others. That concern and love is often transferred visualizing. I encourage you to try it.

4. MEDITATION

Another key tool is meditation. Meditation is something the bible speaks of frequently and is a marvelous way to solidify your faith. Believe it or not, we all meditate. That's what worry is... mulling over and over the negative thing we fear will or won't happen. Remember what you focus on will expand!

Meditating on the positive words of God, His love and provision will make you feel more secure, energetic, and creative. In the book of Joshua, God instructs Joshua to meditate on His Word. Again, what we focus on expands. Meditation empowers us to do as God commands, making us more effective, productive, and courageous. "Meditate ... for then you shall make your way prosperous, and then you shall deal wisely and have good success."[19]

5. KEEP A JOURNAL AND
RECORD WHAT HE SHOWS YOU

Keeping a journal will do you well in becoming more convinced. We all tend to forget the things people say to us, the amazing things we see, and how we experience life. Often Peter in his letters remind us that he is repeating himself because we forget.

Journaling will help you remember. You can go back and recall the experiences you've had with God, the words He's told you, the things that have happened. It will bless you all over again, and thus, deepen the level of conviction you have.

God will open your eyes to see things you never have before. Keep your journal handy as you explore your life of favor. Pretty soon you won't be able to resist seeing favor everywhere. It's a beautiful thing!

Prov. 8:35, "For he who finds me finds life and obtains favor from the Lord.

9

RELEASE RESISTANCE

It's hard to believe anyone would resist something as rewarding, enjoyable, and powerful as the favor of God! I mean, who doesn't want to be esteemed, appreciated, and approved of — by God Almighty, no less? Who doesn't want to be in the right place, with the right people, at just the right time? Who doesn't want their life illumined, encompassed, and empowered by good fortune?

We all want that!

But resistance is totally understandable. Something this good is often met with some sort of suspicion.

"Can it be **for me**?" we ask.

And then our brain tries answering this question based on our past experiences, and our existing mindset. We think of all the times when things did not work out for us, or when we prayed for something and didn't see it happen, or when we were hurt by disappointment.

We don't want to get set up again, hoping for something wonderful, only to get slapped down one more time.

Quiet resignation seems like our best option.

And yet, our hearts hope.

As I said earlier, it took a long time for God to convince me that I am favored, wholly and fully loved, and that He delights in teaching me, helping me, doing things for me, and giving to me. When I'd get a new revelation, or see His favor obviously at work, or feel the incredible sensation of being wrapped in His arms, I felt renewed, inspired, and enthused.

In the height of such faith, I'd take on a new project, make steps toward my dreams, or approach my business with sheer joy. I'd get excited and be confident that I was on the right path. But then a little doubt here, a little there, and before I knew it, I'd feel like I was back to square one.

Let me encourage you. If you find the doubts twisting around your hope and squeezing it like a python, remember, God is greater. There is nothing He can't or won't do for you. He is on your side, and pythons are nothing to Him.

There is a verse so familiar to us, that we have to work at not minimizing it, but it was my anchor for months. You know it, I'm sure.

"Are you tired? Worn out? Burned out on religion? Come to me. Get away with me and you'll recover your life. I'll show you how to take a real rest. Walk with me and work with me—watch how I do it. Learn the unforced rhythms of grace. I won't lay anything heavy or ill-fitting on you. Keep company with me and you'll learn to live freely and lightly." (Mt 11:28-30; The Message Bible)

Many people who are worn out, stressed out, and struggling know this verse, and yet don't take advantage of the help offered here.

Don't be like that! This is a promise to you from the One who knows you best.

A loss of hope is one of the heaviest burdens we can have. Living without hope — hope about ourselves, about our relationships, about our businesses, about our future — is an incredibly difficult stress on our lives. And we carry it wherever we go. *Go to Him and let Him refresh you, renew your mind, and fill your heart.*

Doubt doesn't stand a chance.

Doubt wants to rob, stomp on and even, kill your hope. Doubt is the dam in the stream, the mountain in the road, the mud covering our windshield. It will obstruct us completely, hinder our way, or block our vision.

That is why Jesus says, "I tell you the truth, if anyone says to this mountain, 'Go, throw yourself into the sea,' and **does not doubt in his heart but believes** that what he says will happen, it will be done for him." (Mk 11:23)

And in another place, "Truly I say to you, if you **have faith the size of a mustard seed**, you will say to this mountain, 'Move from here to there,' and it will move; and nothing will be impossible to you." (Mt 17:20)

Apparently all we need is faith the size of a mustard seed to do the impossible. But doubt can contaminate and dilute our faith. If faith is a horse, doubt is the rider pulling the reins.

But God can and will help you with your doubt. He will never abandon you, even if you doubt Him.

He wants to change your mind about Him and yourself and what He has in store for you. He wants to energize your hope and help you see what He sees when he looks at you. You are a beauty!

Real change is done by God.

Brain physiologists have recently discovered that our thoughts and memories can actually be seen in our brains; that how we feel about things are merely chemical reactions to our thoughts. And so, by changing our thoughts and beliefs, we can change our feelings. "I can't help how I feel!" is no longer a legitimate stance.

But with thoughts and beliefs so embedded in our brains, how does one actually change them? Indeed, scientists have discovered that when people do try and change, think differently and adopt a new set of beliefs, they will, at first, experience a nothingness. It takes a while for new neural connections to form that will trigger new chemical reactions, and thus, new emotions.

We do not like to feel nothing. Distress is better than nothing. And so, we go back to old patterns. That is more comforting than nothing.

And yet, resurrecting, renewing, or igniting hope requires a change of mind and heart. Thankfully, we have a God who knows us so well, and has the power to create any kind of change — including our minds — and He desires to do so on our behalf.

The message of favor is a message of hope. And on your way to embracing it fully, doubt will come upon you. Don't think there is something wrong with you. Just keep in mind, God is on your side. Stay close to Him, or get more connected to Him, if you feel distant. Christ in you is your hope of glory.

So now, with God on your side, here are some practical steps you can take to participate with Him in releasing old limiting mindsets and developing healthy, positive ones. The good news is – most of these you have already done!

1. **Be open and take steps to learning.** If you picked up this book, not knowing about the favor of God for you personally, you were ignorant. That only means you lacked the knowledge. By reading this, you are positioning yourself for a major mind renewal! "We are transformed by the renewing of our minds." (Ro. 12:1) All the stories, interactive exercises and scriptures are here to help you become educated in the ways of favor, but also to help you see it for yourself. Continue to search out God and His word. He will reinforce and expand what you are learning here.

2. **If the voices of doubt persist, ask God to unmask the liar.** What is that lie that sounds like the truth? This won't happen overnight. It would be too much for you. But as the lies are exposed, trust that it was brought up by God, not to torment you, but to strip it of its power over you.

3. **Once identified, denounce these voices as lies.** Jesus has given you His power and authority to be the boss of them. How do you put down a lie? You SAY yes to truth and no to lies. You SAY you are done with it. You SPEAK what is true instead. In the next chapter I will tell you about a real life example where I was taunted by lies about my son, and what God led me to do about it.

4. **Persevere.** You can develop your faith just like any muscle, increasing its strength and efficiency. If you don't see a

turnaround immediately, keep building your faith, rather than getting into doubt and tearing down what has already been built. Be regular about seeking God, hearing from Him, and reading His promises in the Word. Start your day off with a few affirming statements that agree with God and His plan for you.

5. **Get prayer**. Often we need the help of others to stand with us. Sometimes our negative mindsets become like concrete and we need someone gifted in detonating spiritual bombs to break us free.

6. **Be accountable.** Get a friend or employ a coach to help you stay on track and keep you focused on your goals. Make sure they are someone you respect, trust, and can't push around. Often we choose people who we feel comfortable with, which is fine, but someone that doesn't have the nerve to stand up to us and our whiny ways is not much help. You don't need sympathy. You need strong, loving honesty. There is a tendency to protect the mindsets we have grown accustomed to. It can be scary to let them go.

Listen, all doubt ultimately finds its origin in three basic questions:

- **Did God say ... ?**
- **Does God care?**
- **Am I valuable enough for this good thing?**

We need to be settled on these three things. Know what God says, either directly or through the Word. Trust His character, no matter what you've seen or what you've been taught. Believe and accept you are worthy.

The degree to which you are unsure about any of these things is the degree to which resistance will hinder you.

Michael Oher, Susan Boyle, Joseph , David, and Moses, all had their times of doubt. You will too. You are in good company.

TELL TALE SIGNS

Finally, if you are unsure if you are resistant, (yes, we can be blind to our resistances), here are some tell-tale signs that signal favor has not been embraced and internalized. Upon seeing them, resolve to take them to the Lord and ask for His brilliant insight and wisdom. Ask Him what the truth is so you can begin to stand on it.

Do you ever think or say:

- "Favor sounds great, but not for me!"
- "I have no problem with the favor of God, it's man's favor I'm worried about!" Then you proceed talking about all the things that have happened to you (again), to prove why you feel that way.
- "How come they get that and I don't?"
- You take offense when someone tells you something you already know. "Don't they know I already know that?" And then you just have to say something to show you are already well aware of that information.
- You often feel left out and excluded. You forget the times you have been invited to things, focusing on the times you have not.
- You often think no one likes you and on a rare occasion you will ask someone why that is. But you aren't really asking for an answer. You are really looking for affirmation.

- When things go wrong, again, you might ask your friend if they know why. But any explanation is perceived as a criticism. You're really looking for someone to tell you it's not your fault.

- When something good happens to you, you minimize it, condition it, or throw in something bad to balance the good. A friend may say, "That's great!" But you will add some downside to the blessing. *"Yeah, I'm glad I got the job, but I didn't get paid as much as wanted... or now I have to be there so early.. or..."* Anyone thinking you have a great life would be contrary to how you see it, and somewhere deep inside you need to be right and be a victim. (By the way, victims are given a break. People feel sorry for them, rather than hold them responsible.)

- You have to explain and justify how you feel about everything. Behind the very detailed explanation is the fear, *"I hope you don't judge me... disapprove of me... talk about me to others..."* (Years ago, this was my personal favorite.)

- You take comments made to you and instantly turn it into something about you, or against you. I remember when I was introducing a new business venture to a friend and without really listening to the details, he blurted out, "That's a scam!" I was stunned and went home shell shocked. *"Did he think I was an idiot? Or maybe he thought I was willing to throw years of trust down the drain and con them so I could make a buck or two?"* Rather than see the comment as something about my friend, I made it all about me. I wasted way too much energy stewing about that one.

Now, if you have recognized some of these, take heart. Embracing favor will solve every one of these.

Which of the above tell tale signs are you familiar with?

_____

_____

_____

What will you do about it?

_____

_____

_____

10

EXPECT, DECLARE, AND SHARE

K nowing God intimately, loving Him, and seeing Him as the source of all favor, is the ultimate experience of feeling special and significant. God is thoroughly pleased to lavish you with such goodness.

And as wonderful as that is, there is so much more!

Favor increases when we expect it, declare it and share it. To see it in our daily lives, impacting the lives of others, causing us to be more effective and magnetic, increases our confidence and joy to serve the world and advance the Kingdom. It gives us the ability to see beyond today to the fulfillment of our dreams tomorrow. Mankind, as a whole, is elevated as God's creation, made in His image, through simple acts of favor. Everyone wins.

EXPECT FAVOR!

Expectation is another one of those buzz words that automatically triggers a response. It either calls forth excitement or offense.

Well, if there is any concern, let me reassure you: I am not suggesting anyone be like a demanding, spoiled child. To me, expectation is a positive state of mind, which agrees with God at His word. *If He says I am favored, then I am favored. If He says I can expect favor wherever I go, then I expect favor wherever I go. See?*

Favor is meant to be more than a warm fuzzy, as delightful as that is. It is meant to produce results in our lives. As you saw from the previous examples, typically favor changes lives!

One of my sisters recently noticed that since my transformation into favor, I care less about the backlash of others. Being the perpetual people pleaser, who worried too much about what others thought of me, this was great news! Indeed, it isn't that I don't care what people think, I'm just not worried anymore about how their opinion can hurt me.

Additionally, I believe more than ever that I can walk into any situation and somewhere I will see favor.

A few years ago my husband, our youngest son, Joe, and I went to Tennessee for a Writer's Conference for homeschooling parents and their teens. The drive was long and arduous. We arrived at the hotel around 11 pm, registered and met with our host. I, along with Joe, could not help but notice the rude, undisguised once-overs that he was receiving. The rejection in their eyes took me by surprise and stabbed me in my heart for him.

True, we were in a very conservative part of the country, at a conference with a very conservative group of people, and he was wearing a black hooded sweatshirt, black chained pants, and his hair had a large red swatch prominently displayed. One might ask, "Well, what did you expect?"

Well, because of what the Lord has taught me, I no longer expect rejection, regardless of it flying at us like heat-seeking missiles.

Joe wanted to leave in the morning, and I didn't blame him. My husband said we'd decide in the morning, but my mind was already made up. I'm as much a mama bear as the next mother. No way was I going to let my son be subjected to this kind of treatment for three days. I went to bed, but barely slept.

"Why does he **always** have to encounter these reactions? Why can't people just accept and love one another? They're so stupid! Arghh...!" I complained bitterly.

After tossing and turning for several hours, I heard the Lord say loud and clear, "You know what to do."

Like the light bulbs in the cartoons, one went off in my brain, and I repeated, "I know what to do."

Have you ever seen the second *Star Wars* movie? Obiwan is in a bar and this guy asks him, "Do you want to buy some death sticks?"(cigarettes)

Obiwan: "You don't want to sell me death sticks."

Guy: "I don't want to sell you death sticks."

Obiwan: "You want to go home and rethink your life."

Guy: "I want to go home and rethink my life."

I love that part. It was like Obiwan just took over the guy's brain.

That was how this felt. And so, repeating God's word to me, just as if it were my own, I jumped out of bed, and paced the room declaring with supernatural faith:

"My son was not created for rejection! My son is favored by God, made with a purpose, destined to prosper and impact this world. He is accepted in the Beloved, esteemed and cherished by God Almighty. He belongs here. He deserves to learn without hindrance. I denounce unworthiness, rejection, discrimination, or judgment. I thank You Lord for being here and for what You will be doing in this place!" *(These were all truths I had previously studied and accepted, but had forgotten under the circumstances.)*

I went to bed, knowing God had directed me to stake a claim in that place. I slept like a baby.

The next morning, we decided to stay and after registration, went to breakfast. Little did we know, we would be treated with the most breathtaking view of the Smoky Mountains. Joining hands to pray, our connection with the Lord seemed extra strong and special. I felt grateful.

Right after, a woman a couple of tables away, thanked us for listening in on our prayer. We exchanged some basic pleasantries, when she asked us why we were there. We told her, and she said she was there for the same reason as well. Cool. But she wasn't a mere attendee … she was the main speaker, author Nancy Rue.

Amazing. Favor. The interesting thing is, she directed almost all her conversation to Joe. "I love those pants, Joe. Do they jingle when you walk? I love that patch of red in your hair. It's just the right amount to make it look interesting without overpowering … Say, what'd you think about that scenery coming up? Did it make you think of a scary setting in a horror story?" And on and on, they shared tips and ideas.

Later at the seminar, Nancy was teaching on the concept of setting in creating a story. Didn't she refer to her conversation with Joe, her new friend, and ask him to stand up? For the next three days, the boy that everyone glared at **"found favor in their sight."**

Quite a lesson to me, **expecting and asserting favor <u>in faith</u> has more power than rejection**. We could feel an actual, tangible shift in the very atmosphere of that place. God's truth, rightfully declared is powerful.

Since then, I proclaim favor for me and others whenever I go into a new environment. Whether for business or social, I expect favor and I say so.

DECLARE FAVOR!

Maybe you aren't sure speaking truth out loud has any real impact. Maybe you are embarrassed to do so. Well let me encourage you. In the *Resource section* of my website I have listed a number of books that will help you understand the power of our words, and why speaking what is true is so important. If you have doubt about the efficacy of speaking faith words, take some time to educate yourself and gain confidence.

As you saw in my example with our son, Joe, speaking truth and not accepting lies created an energy shift in the very air in that place on our behalf!

Another time Joe had a high fever that had lasted way too long, and so, I spoke to it. I knew Jesus had done that with Peter's mother in law, and I knew He had given us the power and authority to do even greater things than He. However, I didn't really believe that I might be able to do just as He did. But one night, faith came and I said, "Fever, go! This body will function as it is made to. Be well, in the name of Jesus."

Within an hour, Joe's temperature dropped almost four degrees. By morning it was normal.

God has given us more power than we know what to do with! And many times it comes out of our mouths!

If you have a business that is faltering – speak words of life, favor, and prosperity over it.

Ps 35:27 says, "The Lord be magnified; Who delights in the prosperity of His servant." God wants you prosperous! He loves you to be successful! So say this is the morning:

- The Lord is on my side.
- I have a thriving, successful business.
- New customers are waiting for me.
- I have a product(s) or service that people need and want.
- I have the favor of God and man wherever I go.
- I am blessed to be a blessing. I spread good will through my business.
- I am creative, intelligent, and ethical.
- God has made me strong, vibrant, and wise.

Do you see? Don't speak words that are not true. Speak that which agrees with God, even if you are not seeing or feeling evidence or manifestation yet.

Truth is what God says and thinks, which is: We bear the image of Almighty God, the Master Creator lives in us. We are a delight to Him, He doesn't see sin when He looks at us, He sees beauty, glory, and His perfection, we have been made whole, right, and powerful, etc. If we speak out truth, in faith, we will see things change for our good.

Lies, on the other hand, come from the author of lies — the evil one. They are accusing, damning, hopeless, and defeating words. 'You can't…you never…you don't…you're never going to succeed because you are defective …you're a fool for thinking you can start a business…people don't care, etc.' Even writing those words affects me. Yuck!

Remember – God created the heavens and the earth by imagining them, then speaking them into existence. That is His way of doing things. Follow it. It's lots easier than all the striving to make things happen that we normally do!

"Death and life are in the power of the tongue, and those who love it will eat its fruit" (Proverbs 18:21)

HERE ARE SOME OTHER DECLARATIONS TO SAY THAT WILL HELP YOU

The Lord surrounds me with His favor like a shield. (Psalm 5:12)

His favor lasts a lifetime. (Ps. 30:5)

He favors me and it makes my mountain stand firm (Ps. 30:7)

I delight myself in the Lord and in His word, and I meditate on Him, therefore I am like a tree planted by streams of water. I produce good fruit! In whatever I do, I prosper. (Ps. 1:2-3)

I am a beaming, radiating center of love, goodness, and wisdom! God lives in me, and I in Him.

Choose three affirmations to speak each day:

1._____

2._____

3._____

God loves you!

SHARE IT!

There are many ways to share favor with the world. That's what the Tuohy family did with Michael Oher. I believe part of loving your neighbor as yourself is extending favor, one to another.

- **Go back through the definitions** of favor and ask, "Who can I treat kindly today? Can I do someone a favor?"

- **Encourage and Elevate.** When we are secure and feel esteemed, we are more apt to encourage and elevate others. Even if you are not yet feeling secure, be generous with your compliments. Recognize the good things people around you do and tell them. Promote them to others. Don't worry about them getting a big head or feeding their ego. Don't worry about them getting the promotion because of your efforts, and you lose out. Trust God and His ways. God wants us to lift each other up. That is His nature and we bear His image. Develop an abundant mindset. There's more than enough for everyone!

- **Tell others what favor has done for you.** The word says we overcome evil by the blood of the Lamb and the word of our testimony. That means when we share what God has done for us, we are literally overcoming negativity, doubt, fear – all the forces of darkness. God has already done His part — our part is merely to share.

Sharing favor is fun. People get blessed, and so will you. Use your mouth and your money to plant seeds of goodness in others' lives. It will come back to you in much greater measure than you gave it.

Feel free to share on my website as well:
www.HaveIEverToldYou.com.
I would love to hear what is happening in your life!

CONCLUSION

B eing favored by God, once believed and accepted, gives us every reason to feel special. Feelings follow belief, and belief follows knowledge. This little book has hopefully served to provide you with that knowledge through stories and scripture, so your eyes will be opened to the world of favor. It has been my goal to help you to know what favor is, so you can believe it for yourself. God wants you to feel special, and hopefully I have been a voice from Him to help convince you. This book is just a start to your journey — the real transforming work will be between you and God.

FEELING SPECIAL IS A NECESSITY OF LIFE

Feeling special has an immensely positive impact on our lives and the lives of those around us. When we feel special, we feel loved and significant. Feeling special produces secondary feelings, like happiness, joy, peace, and contentedness. It gives us a youthful, invigorating outlook about life. It opens our hearts and minds to hope, possibilities, creativity, and generosity. It attracts even more favor!

A positive view of ourselves gives us a greater ability to learn, retain knowledge, and apply wisdom. It allows us to acknowledge our weaknesses without letting those weaknesses define us or get us down. It helps us to comprehend how it is possible to "be of good cheer," when we are faced with trials, tribulations, and the pressures of life.

Furthermore, feeling special is a highly positive emotion that can keep us healthier, and even undo the damaging cardiovascular effects produced by prior negative mindsets. It is healing!

How do we go from a generally negative view of ourselves to a positive one?

First, we need a good, solid reason to believe we are special and favored. Thankfully we can look beyond pop psychology and our own minds for that reason. By the authority of God, we have that reason: **He says so.** Now we have something real and unshakeable upon which we can stand.

The favor of God is a stable, vibrant condition of our lives; something we don't have to perform for. It is an active operating force in our daily affairs, it is how God views us, and it has at its source, His love and approval. Favor makes us feel pretty darn special. However, we need to ask God to open our eyes to it. Opening our eyes to favor will cause us to feel it within, and see it operating in our memories, our daily life, and in our future.

As you consider favor, doubts will arise causing a resistance within you. Welcome that awareness, and release the doubts. I've provided many different avenues by which you can approach God and have quality time with Him. Doing so will cause many of those doubts to naturally melt away.

We can further increase our experience of favor by embracing it, soaking it in, with full appreciation to our God. It is a humbling thing to be so aware of God's constant touch in our lives.

We can also increase the power of favor by expecting it, declaring it over your situation and on behalf of others, and sharing it with those around you. How wonderful is life when we are generously extending the favor of God!

BEGIN A FAVOR REVOLUTION!

Ask God to heighten your awareness of the beauty, preciousness, and capacities you see in others that they may not see in themselves. Be an ambassador of favor! Help people to see that favor comes from God, that He believes in them, and that He has created them uniquely. Listen to people for clues that reveal their God-given dreams and desires, and reflect them back so they can see it.

And don't ever forget … Favor and peace are multiplied very simply – in the true, intimate, and deeply satisfying knowledge of God and our Lord, Jesus. The Spirit of God will transform your life by renewing your mind.

… **Allow the Lord's favor to transform you.**

KEYNOTES AND WORKSHOPS

Whatever the topic, Maryann has a wealth of stories, many humorous, many poignant to illustrate the marvelous workings of God in our lives. Participants find themselves laughing, crying, and often both at the same time.

Through on the spot interactive exercises, all participants are given the opportunity to solidify the things Maryann teaches. Each talk or workshop is designed to have them experience God, His love, His power, and His favor in fresh, revelatory, and transforming ways.

TOPICS

Have I Ever Told You, You're My Favorite?

This topic lends itself well to either a morning breakfast or a two day workshop, preferably in a spa resort type of setting. Maryann has done both. If the workshop mode is chosen, there are two halves:

1. The first half enlivens participants to the availability and operation of favor for them.

2. The second half employs powerful, engaging interactive exercises to enhance participants' experience with God, see themselves through His eyes of favor, and learn how to live in the reality of it.

Prayer and releasing exercises will be available to help all attendants be rid of limiting beliefs and resistance.

Past participants have claimed this is the most encouraging women's retreat they have ever been on!

Dream Activation

The *Have I Ever Told You, You're My Favorite* workshop is a prerequisite to this workshop. Maryann will review principles of favor, with participants sharing how the favor of God has revealed itself in their lives since the last workshop.

The bulk of this workshop will concentrate on taking stock of each participant's unique preferences, skills, gifts and talents. Together they will uncover faded and unfulfilled dreams, or discover ones never before revealed.

7 Steps to Peace, Power, and Prosperity

This is a 3 session workshop or a 7 week teleseminar series. Each step is designed to help participants tap into a higher, more fulfilling experience with God, hear His voice, and identify and release all hindering obstacles to enjoying His presence. Maryann teaches and gives opportunity to use our God-given imagination to visualize and meditate on Him and His Word. Each participant should come with a set of issues/concerns for which they would like clarification, empowerment, and an action plan.

Esthereal Encounter

This workshop employs a totally different approach to exploring the concepts of favor. Using the book of Esther, participants discover the ancient practice of favor. They see the benefits, the operation, and the result of this powerful force, and watch it unfold in their own life. Participants are positioned for courage to rise, vision to be clarified, and the wisdom to make the next steps.

From Frustration to Fabulous

Jesus said that He came to give life, and give it to the full. Abundant life is His idea, His mission, and His way for us. Most Christians know this. Even so, a fabulous life of fullness and favor seems to elude many, experiencing instead, disappointment, frustration and even, failure. Having grown up with abuse, abandonment, and discrimination, Maryann knows personally the struggle to believe God, as well as seeing this struggle in the lives of those she has counseled and coached for almost 30 years.

But God is faithful, and over the years, He has revealed 3 Key Truths that has turned her life, and the lives of others, from frustration to fabulous! In her message, Maryann will not only share these revelations, but her secret weapon which has helped to bring these truths into practical, daily manifestation.

COACHING PROGRAMS

On Maryann's website, www.HaveIEverToldYou.com you will find a variety of coaching programs, group or private. Check them out and see how she can help you!

BONUS

As a thank you for reading this book, I would love to give you a discount on *7 Steps To Peace, Power, And Prosperity–Inspired Results From The Heart Of God.*

Go to www.HaveIEverToldYou.com/7steps

ABOUT THE AUTHOR

Maryann's expertise is people. Since childhood she has been a keen observer, attentive listener, and compassionate helper. She has an uncanny gift from God to hear hidden pains, secret dreams, and wisdom from above. Passionate about helping people find their true selves, their authentic value and worth, and the reason for their being, Maryann has helped countless of individuals, couples, and families find peace with God, acceptance of themselves, and fulfillment in their relationships. Whether sitting in the boardroom, courtroom, or classroom, for Maryann it has always been about people.

Maryann has a B.S. in Elementary Education, Minor in Psychology from SUNY - Geneseo, NY. She taught for several years while working on her Masters from Western Connecticut State University, Danbury, CT. She then earned her J. D., majoring in tax law, from WNEC, School of Law, Springfield, MA. As a lawyer Maryann served as a prosecutor, and a manager for a large financial company, teaching financial principles and designing financial plans. After, Maryann successfully owned and operated her own business as a Financial Consultant to small business owners. She became a Certified Financial Counselor with Christian Financial Concepts, currently Crown Financial Ministries. Maryann has logged in thousands of hours continuing her education in spiritual, financial, and over the last 10 years, natural health related topics.

Maryann homeschooled her children, and continues to assist her husband in his private investigation business. Throughout the years, God has brought to Maryann many to receive recovery and restoration from shame and guilt caused by abuse and rejection issues of all kinds. Passionate about God and His Word, she has lead and taught people in how to read the Bible, apply it personally and practically to every area of their lives, and develop a closer, more intimate connection with their God…the cure for whatever ails us.

Heeding the call of God to write, speak, lead workshops and retreats, Maryann has shifted her work from counseling to coaching. For a number of years now, the Lord has put more entrepreneurial minded people in her path with big dreams that need clarification, activation, and a plan of action. This is a joyful and exciting work! Identifying and releasing obstacles and hindrances internally and externally is her specialty.

Besides all the serious stuff, Maryann loves to cook, travel, go to "chick flicks" with her girlfriends, and basically, enjoy every aspect of life. *A girl's just got to have fun!*

Maryann lives in western New York, smack dab in the middle of 4 lovely acres with her husband Gene. She has four incredibly fascinating children, seven brilliant, funny, and delightful grandsons, and one absolutely darling granddaughter.

FOOTNOTES

[1] Bill Johnson, *Face to Face with God,* Lake Mary, Florida; Charisma House Publishing, p 25

[2] Ibid, p 178

[3] Thankfully I am no longer plagued by the shame and guilt associated with this event, however, it is a huge problem in our country. 1 in 4 girls and 1 in 6 boys have been sexually abused...that we know about. That means there are a lot of people having to deal with shame and guilt, many of whom do not know what to do about this feeling of unworthiness, deficiency, and guilt they carry around with them. Embracing favor is crucial. http://www.cdc.gov/nccdphp/ace/prevalence.htm *ACE Study - Prevalence - Adverse Childhood Experiences*

[4] Dale Carnegie, *How to Win Friends and Influence People,* Pocket, 1st Printing Edition, 2005

[5] Dr. Norman Vincent Peale, *The Power of Positive Thinking,* Fireside Edition, Simon & Schuster, 1990

[6] Bill Johnson, *Face to Face with God*, p 24-25

[7] Genesis 37:3, et seq

[8] Merriam-Webster Collegiate Dictionary; Publisher, Merriam Webster, 10th edition, 1998

[9] Genesis 2:7, et seq

[10] Genesis 1:12

[11] Genesis 1:31

[12] John 10:10

[13] Mt., 19:26

[14] Mt 6:10

[15] Heidi and Rolland Baker, *Expecting Miracles*, Publisher, Chosen, 2007; p 185

[16] *Les Miserables,* Claude-Michel Schönberg (music), Alain Boublil (lyrics), 1980

Maryann Ehmann, BS, JD
119

[17] Here is favor for Audra Mae, the author of this song, too. Audra wrote this song after researching Susan's story. Struggling for years in the songwriting business, Audra never expected the song to receive the accolades it has. By the way, Audra is the grandniece of Judy Garland. http://www.susanboylemusic.com/nl/forum/viewthread/76430/

[18] *Susan Boyle and the Love of God,* American Magazine, James Martin, S.J., 4/16/2009.

[19] Joshua 1:8, *Amplified Bible*, Zondervan Publishing, 2001